LIVING TRUE

LIVING TRUE

COLLEEN EVANS

While this book is designed for the reader's personal enjoyment and profit, it is also intended for group study. A Leader's Guide with Victor Multiuse Transparency Masters is available from your local bookstore or from the publisher.

VICTOR

BOOKS a division of SP Publications, Inc.
WHEATON, ILLINOIS 60187

Offices also in
Whitby, Ontario, Canada
Amersham-on-the-Hill, Bucks, England

Recommended Dewey Decimal Classification: 227.91
Suggested Subject Heading: BIBLE. N.T. JAMES; SPIRITUAL LIFE

Library of Congress Catalog Card Number: 84-52040
ISBN: 0-89693-321-0

VICTOR BOOKS A division of SP Publications, Inc.
Wheaton, Illinois 60187

CONTENTS

Acknowledgments 6

Introduction 8

 1 **James Who?** 12

 2 **Working Through the Tough Times** 20

 3 **Don't Blame God** 30

 4 **True Religion: Where the Rubber Meets the Road** 40

 5 **No Snobbery Allowed** 52

 6 **Possessed by Possessions or Stewards of God?** 66

 7 **Faith & Works: Not Either/Or, but Both!** 82

 8 **The Tongue: Troublemaker or Transformed by God?** 94

 9 **Slander & Judgment** 106

10 **God's Peace—For the Heart and for the World** 118

11 **Humility** 130

12 **Church Alive: Praying, Praising, Anointing, and Reaching Out** 140

ACKNOWLEDGMENTS

Through the years of my Christian life, James has been more than a favorite New Testament book for me; it has been close to an obsession. The predictable practicality of its teaching has lured me to buy books, attend retreats, enroll in classes—and now, try my hand at writing on James myself.

But before you read what I have to say, I want to make it very clear that I've had help—lots of it! Over the years I have gleaned many ideas from others about the Book of James; those ideas have become a part of my thinking, and will be found on the pages that follow.

Specifically, two volumes come to mind that were of tremendous help in my studies: William Barclay's *Daily Study Bible* (Westminster Press) and Derek Prime's *From Trials to Triumph.*

I wish I could give credit to every person whose spoken or written words gave me a fresh idea, or whose scholarship sent me searching in a new direction—but I can't. My "rememberer" just isn't that good...or my notes that complete. Just know that I am indebted to a host of people—even if I can't remember all of your names.

But there are some people who have helped me with this

project of whom I am very aware indeed! First, my father-in-law, the late Dr. Louis Evans, Sr. Many years ago Dad wrote a book titled, *Make Your Faith Work,* and the way in which he systematized the recurring themes of James into chapters helped me tremendously in my initial stage of organization.

Second, the late Dr. Frank Gaebelein, a cherished friend to me and my husband. Dr. Gaebelein's books, *Faith That Lives* and *The Expositors Bible* on James (which he edited), were of enormous help. In fact, you will find them quoted many times in this book.

And finally, our daughter Andie Evans Goodrich, who typed, and encouraged, and lent her considerable editing gifts to "Mom's project."

My deep thanks to these three very special people who have each held—and continue to hold—a unique place in my heart.

INTRODUCTION

There is something nourishing about simplicity, living without the frills. Perhaps that's why my husband and I are called back year after year to this place we love so much. At this moment, I am perched on a steep hillside above a glacier-fed lake in the High Sierra of California. Louie and I are here alone for a time of rest and renewal. It is here that the Lord, quite literally, "makes us to lie down in green pastures (meadows?) and restores our souls" for the next year's work. And so it has been for the past 20 years, and more.

In a week our family will arrive, complete with backpacks, busy agendas and friends . . . lots of friends! The tempo and mood will change. It will be warm and rich, noisy and chaotic, and I will love it. I always do. But for now, my soul is drinking in the goodness of the quiet and simplicity of these days.

Here in the mountains, even our mealtimes are dictated by the vacation spirit. In Washington, the dinner hour is squeezed in between the last appointment of the afternoon and the beginning of the evening meeting. Eating is an accommodation ruled by the clock. But when Louie and I are alone in the Sierra, meals happen only when we want them to. On a certain day we may swim and sun so long that we become famished, and so the snacks that we keep in the shade at the water's edge become a meal, and dinner that night is simply forgotten. Another day we may both be so involved in our projects that we remember to eat only when the pangs of hunger remind us. Then we gather wood, light a fire, wait for the coals to turn just the right shade of gray and spend the last hours of our day barbecuing a simple meal and relishing every tasty bite. It's a splendid way to live, if only for a few weeks of every year. It's a time of returning to the basics—a "meat and potatoes" kind of existence, which not only feels good to my body, but, in some way, cleanses and nourishes my soul as well.

That's much the same way I feel about the Book of James, however unlikely the comparison might be. I have loved this book since I first became a Christian and discovered that its "meat and potatoes" religion was food for my soul. And through the years its practical teaching on "faith that works" has called me back many times to the basics of Christian living. Like the High Sierra, a return to James refreshes my spirit again and again.

The late Dr. J.B. Phillips said:

> Paul taught that a person was "justified" not by
> achievement but by a real faith. James says that the test
> of a real faith is whether it issues in appropriate
> behavior.

And, of course, Paul and James both spoke the truth. If we are biblical Christians, we do not have the luxury of choosing one or the other. When it comes to faith or works, it is not a matter of "either-or," but "both-and." It is precisely this insistence on "both-and" that makes the epistle such an important book for us.

Not everyone places such high value on the Book of James. Some think it is so lacking in doctrinal content that they regard it as unworthy of serious study. Nor is this idea original. Over 450 years ago Martin Luther made his feelings known in typically blunt fashion when he dubbed

James "the epistle of straw." Yet in 2 Timothy 3:16-17, we read that all Scripture is profitable "for teaching, rebuking, correcting and training in righteousness, so that the man of God may be thoroughly equipped for every good work."

It is true that James doesn't center on doctrine, but in terms of "rebuking, correcting and training in righteousness" it is absolutely bursting with practical knowledge and help. In fact, if we study and apply what we learn to everyday life, I am convinced we will grow in maturity and be "thoroughly equipped for every good work."

I have always wanted to spend a year in the Book of James, then write a study for women who, like me, want to grow in maturity and the living out of their faith. Needless to say, I am grateful to the people at Victor Books, especially Jim Adair, for giving me this opportunity and encouraging me to do it *now.* Furthermore, I believe Christian women are dissatisfied with the abundance of spiritual "froth" available to them and are increasingly hungry for content and practical help. James is overflowing with both.

I am well into my year of study as I write this introduction. However, it has been very difficult to get a handle on this epistle, and nearly an impossibility to outline it. Someone has described James as "less a train of thought than a string of pearls," and so I have found it to be. Recently, I was greatly encouraged to find that the late Dr. Frank Gaebelein, a dear friend and biblical scholar, felt the same way:

> What James wrote under the inspiration of the Spirit of
> God is not so much a reasoned argument as a series of
> sententious sayings clustered around certain recurring
> themes (*Faith That Lives,* Moody Press).

Much relieved after reading Dr. Gaebelein's words, I stopped trying to analyze and outline James and began studying it as a living letter that confronted me with powerful ethical implications of the Gospel. *Then* I found I could identify those "recurring themes" and collate those "sententious sayings" into chapters that satisfied my need for order.

As I expected, God is using this study to make me stretch toward new areas of credibility in my own Christian life. Such growth isn't always comfortable, but it is deeply satisfying—the way a simple meal is satisfying when you are very hungry. And as I said earlier, James portrays a "meat and potatoes" faith. If we appropriate this nutritious spiritual food into our lives, we will come closer to being the women God created us to be. Then we cannot help but make a difference in the world for Him.

I am excited. I hope you are too.

COLLEEN EVANS

James, the slave of God and of the Lord Jesus Christ, sends greetings.

ONE
JAMES WHO?

It was a crisp, clear winter morning in Washington. Even I, who am definitely *not* an early morning person, had to admit it was beautiful. It was 7:15, and I was on my way to Fellowship House to join a group of friends concerned about our inner city. We would breakfast together, then have a time of prayer and planning. Excited about being part of such a gathering, I nevertheless had to grumble a bit to my husband, Louie, who *is* a morning person. "Why do so many godly things go on in Washington at such *un*godly hours?" I asked. He smiled.

After we arrived and I had my first cup of coffee, I was nicer—even *glad* to be there.

We sat around an oblong table in the sunny alcove of the lovely old dining room, eating, praying, and conducting our business. But the highlight of the morning came when our work was done and one of our members began to share, warmly and informally, his family history.

Ernest, a deeply respected minister of the Gospel here in Washington, D.C., told us his grandparents had been slaves. They were totally at the disposal of their master, their lives literally someone else's property. When they were still young, the Civil War changed everything. They were freed

13

and able to determine a new direction for their lives. I was touched as Ernest shared his roots, especially when he spoke about his grandmother and the profound influence she'd had on his life. A woman of deep faith, she taught her children and grandchildren to claim their dignity as children of God. She literally trained Ernest to stand ramrod straight and tall as a sign of that dignity—and at one point in his life, that very characteristic became a problem for him.

While he was a student at Howard University he got a part-time job, which he very much needed, clerking in a men's clothing store. From the beginning, the manager chided him about his dignified stance, and finally fired him, saying, "You stand so straight, our customers think you are 'uppity.' "

Ernest laughs about it now, but at the time it hurt. What a sad commentary on his manager's attitude, which was, in turn, a reflection of much of our society at that time.

I'm glad to say Ernest stands just as tall today—and there is no question about the acceptance of his leadership in our city. In his words, "We still have grave problems that must be faced—and dealt with—*but* we've come a long way." And when we consider the evils of slavery, indeed we have.

No one is meant to own and control another person's life. And when people within families or nations try to do this, it is destructive and dehumanizing. Only God can do that, and win.

William Barclay, in his excellent commentary, says:

> The *love* of God *desires* only what is best for you, the *wisdom* of God *knows* what is best for you, and the *power* of God can *bring about* what is best for you (*The Daily Study Bible,* "The Letters of James and Peter," Revised Edition, Westminster Press).

It was to this loving, all-wise, all-powerful God that *James,* who authored this Bible book, gave his life as a slave. Whoever he was, the very first sentence of his epistle gives us a strong clue as to the kind of character he possessed.

Slave of God and of the Lord Jesus Christ.

With the exception of Jude, this James is the only New Testament writer to describe himself so simply, without qualification. *Doulos,* the word he used for *slave,* implies radical loyalty and submission. It meant he no longer determined the results of his life. He was not in control, for that is the nature of slavery. This was a person abandoned to the service of his Master, an invaluable piece of information for us. But beyond that we still don't know much about *who* James was, except that he was a humble man.

As I looked for more information about the writer of the Book of James, I found various theories. Some scholars say he could have been the son of Alpheus, but so little is written and known about James the son of Alpheus that most scholars agree he is an unlikely candidate. Others think he might have been the brother of John and one of the sons of Zebedee. But in the Gospels, that James never appeared apart from John and, more significantly, he was martyred too early to have written this letter. The most widely endorsed author of this epistle is James, the brother of our Lord. Almost all commentaries favor this theory, and in my view, the evidence given to support it is convincing.

As we read the New Testament, it is clear that Jesus had a brother named James. The Gospel story tells us that Mary gave birth to Jesus, her "firstborn Son" (Luke 2:7, KJV), which certainly indicates that others followed. Jesus was Mary's son by the Holy Spirit; James was Mary's son by Joseph; or, to use a technical term, they were *uterine* brothers (Mark 6:3; Matt. 13:55).

Jesus' family did not always understand Him. In fact, once His public life began, their response to His ministry was often less than enthusiastic (Matt. 12:46-50; Mark 3:21, 31-35; John 7:3-9). John 7:5 says bluntly, "Even His own brothers did not believe in Him." So as Jesus walked this earth, ministering and calling people to His new kingdom, James was not one of those who followed. We could understand if James, as a younger brother, was a little annoyed, perhaps even apologetic, about his older brother's involvements, the company He kept and the offbeat places He was seen. Given James' background as a devout Jew and his Hebrew concept of the kingly Messiah, it is not surprising that the simplicity of Jesus' life confirmed James' skepticism regarding his brother's divinity.

But, this is not the end of the story, of course. As with many of us who did not early come to Christ, something powerful happened—and it changed everything for James. First Corinthians 15:7 alludes to this experience when Paul gives a list of resurrection appearances of Jesus, and says, "Then He appeared to James." What happened between James and the Risen Christ in those moments we can only guess. But the fact remains that after their encounter, James was never the same again. At first an unsympathetic younger brother, James ultimately became Jesus' *doulos*—His servant-slave—for the rest of his life.

When the Acts of the Apostles opens, James then is one of the members of the faithful band (Acts 1:14). From then on, it is clear that he is the leader of the first body of believers in Jerusalem. In fact, James presided over the Council of Jerusalem when the decision was made to allow Gentiles into the church fellowship (Acts 15:1-21).

Early church historians also help us get to know this brother of Jesus as they describe James' character and devotion:

> Alone he would enter the temple, and be found prostrate on his knees beseeching pardon for the people, so that his knees were callous like a camel's in consequence of his continual kneeling in prayer to God. . . . Because of his exceeding righteousness he was called the Just (Hegesippus, *Ecclesiastical History,* 2:23).

The historian Josephus spoke briefly of James' death by stoning (*Antiquities,* 20:9.1). Though James may have been slow to embrace his brother as the Messiah, he ultimately died a martyr's death for Him.

There is more that we know about James. Unlike Paul, James did not travel, but stayed in Jerusalem to lead the church and become its first bishop. He must have been a natural leader, for he assumed that role almost instantly in the newborn community of faith. Apparently, he was also the one to whom Christians flocked for counsel (Gal. 1:19—2:9; Acts 21:18-25). As the undisputed leader of the Jewish segment of the church, it would have been natural for him to speak to all Jewish Christians "scattered abroad" in a general epistle like the Book of James.

However, not all New Testament scholars agree that James actually *wrote* the letter given his name. In William Barclay's opinion, the epistle began as a sermon preached by James in Jerusalem. Barclay points out that the letter was written in classical Greek, and that quite certainly James' mother tongue was Aramaic and *not* Greek; and quite certainly he would not be a master of classical Greek. From this, Barclay speculates that James preached the message, that someone present wrote it down, and that it was later translated into Greek so that it could be sent to the church at large "so all people could be helped by its wisdom and power." But whether the epistle we have today began as a letter or a sermon, of this I am sure: It is a message sent from God, and, in my opinion it comes to us through James, who was the brother of our Lord. Beyond that it is a powerful, hard-hitting, and practical message.

- It speaks to the most vulnerable and delicate issues of life.
- It challenges attitudes, actions, and value systems.
- It is as practical today as it was nearly 2,000 years ago.

And it is so needed! We live in an age in which the world is constantly watching those of us who are called by His name to see if our beliefs really make a difference in our lives. It is absolutely crucial that our religion be more than theological principles and dogma: it must be a demonstration as well! The Epistle of James teaches us how this can be, as the brother of our Lord leads us with a firm, yet loving hand into faith that pulses with practical application.

Consider it pure joy, my brothers and sisters*, whenever you face trials of many kinds, because you know that the testing of your faith develops perseverance. Perseverance must finish its work so that you may be mature and complete, not lacking anything. If any of you lacks wisdom, he should ask God, who gives generously to all without finding fault, and it will be given to him. But when he asks, he must believe and not doubt, because he who doubts is like a wave of the sea, blown and tossed by the wind. That man should not think he will receive anything from the Lord; he is a double-minded man, unstable in all he does.

---

*I've taken the liberty of including "sisters" throughout the Scripture quotes from James, for I feel certain he was including both men and women. A detailed explanation is given in chapter 8, page 95.

TWO

WORKING THROUGH
THE TOUGH TIMES

After the simplest of greetings (1:1), James says, "Consider it pure joy my brothers and sisters whenever you face trials of many kinds" (v. 2). Characteristically, he rejects small talk and immediately sets the tone for his letter. In these few words James makes it clear that those who choose to be disciples of his brother, Jesus, must break away from the normally accepted responses to life's problems. James urges his readers to an unusual quality of response; those who follow his advice will distinguish themselves markedly from those who would respond in purely human ways. And these Christians will certainly fit the label "God's peculiar people."

To be joyful about the positive, bright areas of life is no more than one would expect. But to have joy in the midst of real struggle is not natural; it requires a very unique kind of faith and trust. Only as Christ lives within us do we grow into that kind of understanding as part of faith's maturing. And this is one goal James had in mind as he wrote this letter. He encouraged believers to move beyond their immediate human reactions and grow up in faith in Jesus Christ.

A Painful Season

> Consider it pure joy my brothers and sisters whenever
> you face trials of many kinds (v. 2).

Whenever I hear these words I think back to a season of
my life that began almost ten years ago. We had just moved
to Washington, D.C. where Louie had been called to serve
the congregation at the National Presbyterian Church. One
of the resources we both knew we needed was a support
group made up of people who we could trust and who
would be honest enough with us to hold us accountable in
our Christian walk. We prayed earnestly that God would
lead us to those who had the same desires and needs, and in
His own way and time, He did—beyond our expectations.

Part of His answer for me came as I got to know and then
met once a week with a small group of women. Though our
personalities varied greatly, we were alike in one fundamental way. Each of us was hungry for a new depth of relationship with Christ, and we longed for a sisterhood among
ourselves that would offer mutual commitment and support. Little did we know in those first few hours together
how deep—and sometimes costly—the covenant we desired would be.

Week by week we met and slowly unveiled our inner
selves. As we shared our joys, interests, hurts, and fears, our
love and trust began to grow. Not long after, we decided to
incorporate teaching from Scripture into our time together,
and the Letter of James was our choice.

As I think back to that day, it seems we had no sooner
opened our Bibles to the Book of James when verse 2 of the
first chapter jumped out at us and stopped us right in our
tracks:

Count it all joy whenever you face trials of many kinds.

That single verse held us for many weeks. We questioned
its meaning and, more importantly, its meaning questioned
us. We looked honestly at the tendency within each of us to
put on a happy front while seething with resentment inside
because of some "undeserved" trial. Of course, God was not

telling us to be insincere in any way; and so, we reasoned, the verse must mean just what it said. *Somehow* genuine joy was to emerge from our trials; *how* this could be was the thorny question we wrestled with as a group.

Little did we know how soon this truth would be tested by experience; within our small group "various trials" would come to each person in a sobering way. Family death, life-threatening disease, surgery, a prison sentence for one member's spouse (it was the year of Watergate), a lost election (also a fallout from Watergate), a runaway child, and more. No one was exempt.

I remember well my own personal agony—not as dramatic as what some of my sisters were experiencing—but very real to me. In accepting the call to Washington, we had to leave our two older sons in California. One had just begun his first year at the University of California, and the other was in his last year of high school. There was no way we would expect them to tag along with us at that point in their schooling, so we arranged for them to live with a family that was special to all of us. But neither Louie nor I knew how hard it would be to leave Dan and Tim behind. As we drove out of La Jolla, our car loaded with our two younger children, our two dogs, and everything that didn't quite make it into the moving van, Louie and I were quiet—and tearful—as we headed East. Our comfortable and complete nest was being rearranged—never to be exactly the same again.

Of course, I knew that day was coming. But I had not expected it to come so quickly, nor had I expected so many miles to separate us when it *did* arrive. Most of all, I had no idea I would miss Dan and Tim the way I did. I still remember the ache I felt, and, despite all my efforts, the tears that welled up whenever someone asked how the boys were doing "way out there in California."

No doubt about it, my first year in Washington was a tender time. Much of what I knew about myself was suddenly called into question, because my family had been the means by which I had learned most about who I was. As its form began to change, I felt somewhat adrift—needing to get in touch with the self that was on the brink of a new season.

Louie and our two younger children, Andie and Jamie, were a big part of that process; so were my covenant sisters who had become an extended family to me. Together, they helped me see that while I am—and always will be—part of a family that I love, I am also distinct from my family. By encouraging me to develop new gifts for a new season, and supporting me as I tested and tried new ventures, they helped me get in touch with that self that is separate, yet united with another. I will always be grateful.

Of course, it wasn't *all* trauma and pain. For some in our group there were incredibly sweet successes, so we shared joy as well as pain. The more we shared, the closer we grew as our covenant to support one another was called into service—and tested—again and again. As we lived and worked through those eventful months with God and with one another, we returned to James 1:2 many times. We no longer questioned intellectually *how* it could be, but knew in our hearts that it simply *was*.

No Untouchables

A final word on this theme is one, perhaps, of caution. James is offering no tidy solution here to help Christians avoid life's pain and struggle. The "trials of many kinds" are not something from which Christians are immune. They engulf us in the same emotions and temptations as they engulf unbelievers. Our resources for dealing with the trials and all that follows, however, make all the difference.

Recently, I read about the experience of an acquaintance Louie and I have admired for years. His little girl, Lisa, was diagnosed as having Wilm's tumor, a congenital form of children's cancer. In the midst of her treatment for this cruel disease, our friend found himself angered by the responses of many Christians who sought to soothe his agony with spiritual platitudes, or, most disturbing, the belief that this cancer had been "sent" by God to bring about some good. He refused to accept the notion of a God who brought evil upon His people. He explained, "If God is God, then surely He has infinite means at His disposal to accomplish good other than giving innocent children catastrophic illnesses" (Mike Yaconelli, "The Nightmare of a God Who Did It," *The Wittenburg Door,* August-September 1983, p. 3).

Lisa's parents were not compelled to find the "answer" to her illness because they accepted the fact that unwarranted trials inevitably fall upon Christians' lives. Rather, they found their comfort and joy in a God who is the giver and sustainer of life: "In [God's] hand is the life of every creature and the breath of all mankind. . . . For in Him we live and move and have our being" (Job 12:10; Acts 17:28). They fought together with Him to bring health and wholeness back to Lisa's little body.

Ben Patterson, a fellow pastor with whom Louie served in La Jolla, describes well the hazards and the promises of Christian living:

> God nowhere promises understanding or comprehension of it all in the here and now. He nowhere promises that if you do everything right and keep your nose clean that He will shield you from all evil. What He does promise is the presence of His Spirit to uphold and to comfort us. Paul calls Him the "Father of compassion and the God of all comfort, who comforts us in all our troubles, so that *we can comfort* those in any trouble with the comfort we ourselves have received from God" (2 Cor. 1:3-4). (From *The Wittenberg Door,* August-September 1983, p. 34.)

This is joy—not what one could call happiness, and certainly not giddiness or absence of pain—but deep, profound joy in the comfort of God's Spirit through every conceivable trial . . . and the promise that our pain will prove useful as we minister to others in pain.

Growth through Pain

You know that the testing of your faith develops perseverance. Perseverance must finish its work so that you
may be mature and complete, not lacking anything (vv.
3-4).

Without qualification James was stating that our trials
could be used to develop character—and we in our covenant group found his words to be true in our various struggles. Part of our joy *was* in the fact that God was not only
enabling us to *endure* our trials, but that He was actually
using them to bring about new growth in our lives. Pain
and adversity, we learned, were not signs of God's disapproval anymore than success and prosperity were signs of
His approval. We were God's workmanship, and He was
molding us for His use.

In the years since that little group began, remarkable personal growth and creative ministries have arisen out of our
sharing together, not to mention the warm and lasting
friendships.

Two of our members felt called to minister within the
church and have completed seminary degrees. One of them
finished college in her 40s and earned a double masters in
religion and psychology after she was 50. She now heads
the counseling center at National Presbyterian Church. Another woman started her own real estate business, while
still another went back to school in mid-life to become a
C.P.A. Dee, our expert in homemaking, taught French cooking from her own kitchen and decorated a beautiful retreat
center that serves Christian leaders from all corners of the
world. And in a lighter vein, two of the women fulfilled a
long-time desire when they signed up for a tap-dancing
class that added a lot of fun to their lives. But, most important, every one of us grew in our spiritual inward journey as
God's amazing grace was working in and through our lives.

Supporting one another through the tough times made us
wiser, more joyful people as God swept away the shallows
of our lives. As a result of this experience and others like it,

I am convinced that certain Christian graces come to us *only* through the trying experiences of life. Isn't it clear, then, that our goal as Christians should not be painless success as the world understands it, but *faithfulness* as God perceives it? For it is precisely the trials in life which equip us for such faithfulness and service. As maturing believers, we are called to accept the grace God offers us to be joyful—*even as we hurt.*

Sensible Suffering

As I study James 1:3-4, I find that what my Bible translation calls *perseverance,* another calls *steadfastness,* and still another calls *patience.* Good words, all. *Patience,* however, is the word most familiar to me, so I am inclined to interpret it more superficially. But a closer look shows that this word has more substance than I first thought. In reading my father-in-law's book, I learn that patience comes from two Latin words—*patior* which means, "I suffer," and *sensio* which means, "with sense" (Louis Evans, Sr., *Make Your Faith Work,* Revell). In other words, we face suffering sensibly and meaningfully, and as disciples of Christ we are assured that we never face it alone, but always with His grace.

Two of the dearest, most committed Christians Louie and I know are Michi and Ernest Takeda. Their friendship has blessed us over the years in ways too many to count. The last time we were together in California, sitting around their table devouring huge portions of Michi's delicious chirashi sushi, donburi, and sashimi, the conversation turned to the days of World War II, specifically the Takedas' experiences as Japanese Americans during those painful years. Michi and Ernest recalled how they and their families were interned in a relocation camp in Arkansas when the two of them were still in their teens. In fact, they met there when they both volunteered to teach Sunday School at the improvised Community Christian Church. They spoke of the abrupt uprooting of their happy and productive lives in California and of the emotional pain and material losses of many U.S. citizens of Japanese ancestry during those troubled years. But Louie and I were most deeply impressed with their total absence of bitterness and we questioned them about this. Their response was disarmingly transparent and sincere. Ernest stated simply, "We were Christians," and Michi added, "E. Stanley Jones came to our camp to minister to us, and he taught us not to be bitter." So simple, and so thoroughly Christian! As I ponder the true meaning of patience (to suffer with sense and grace), I think of Michi and Ernest whose lives today beautifully demonstrate the maturity that steadfastness and perseverance can bring when undeserved trials hit.

And how can we think about "undeserved trials" without our hearts aching for our brothers and sisters in Africa who are suffering hunger and starvation because of a drought that has plagued their land year after year.

James was speaking to the same kind of people in his day—people who, through no fault of their own, were being tested and tried every day of their lives. They were people without a country, living in foreign lands. J.B. Phillips calls them the "twelve displaced tribes," and every day brought humiliating reminders that they were a conquered, suffering people. In spite of this, James encouraged them to so live out their trust in Jesus Christ that everyone would know their faith was not merely an opiate or their Christianity a fair-weather religion. Rather, theirs was a commitment to God that gained new strength through trial and struggle, and our commitment should be no less so today.

> *Our Father,*
> *As "various trials" come to each of us, as they surely will, keep us from reacting in a shallow way—as though smooth and happy circumstances are something we are promised, and to which we are somehow entitled, as children of Yours.*
>
> *Rather, help us work through our tough times with perseverance and grace, as we depend upon the Holy Spirit. Convince us, deep in our beings,*

that joy is not the absence of pain, but it is Your presence with us through every circumstance of life.

For this sure promise, we thank You with all our hearts. Amen.

Blessed is the man who perseveres under trial, because when he has stood the test, he will receive the crown of life that God has promised to those who love Him. When tempted, no one should say, "God is tempting me." For God cannot be tempted by evil, nor does He tempt anyone; but each one is tempted when, by his own evil desire, he is dragged away and enticed. Then, after desire has conceived, it gives birth to sin; and sin, when it is full-grown, gives birth to death.

THREE
DON'T BLAME GOD

Many of us who proclaim faith in Jesus Christ try to pin the blame for our trials on the Lord. We complain, *If God is really in control, how could He let this happen?*

How true this is in my own life! I make a thoughtless mistake or willful choice and if the events that follow bring disappointment or trial, I blame God. Certainly many of us have made a habit of doing this. Adam set the precedent. After making his wrong choice, he self-righteously protested before God, "It was the woman *YOU* sent me who made me do it!" Pointing the finger at someone else for our own errors seems to run in the human family.

When we make wrong choices and bellow out at God, we merely reveal our own rebelliousness. We go our own willful ways and when the inevitable occurs, God, the lover of justice and mercy, gets the blame. He hardly has a chance!

What a costly risk God took when He created us with free will. Yet that very free will is the mark of His love, which does not force our love in return. Love is genuine only when it flows freely; it is a voluntary embrace, not a stranglehold. That awesome freedom to choose, James clearly implies, leads either to blessing or condemnation in our lives. Whichever path we take, God stands blameless.

This is truth, and we must accept it. However, it is not *all* of the truth. If we stop here, we will be blind to the full beauty of the Gospel as well as the full message James is communicating. For even when our temptations and trials *are* self-created and centered in sin, the *Good News* is that Jesus pardons our sins if we choose His way. No matter *what* we have done, He is waiting to receive us with His forgiving, unconditional love.

A Matter of Choice

I have a long-time acquaintance who has recently become a real friend. She is someone who has been changed dramatically by God's unconditional love. For years she had been stubbornly defying God by making one willful choice after another, leading to a bad marriage, a self-defeating sexual identity, tragic efforts to escape her problems the "painless" way through alcohol and other drugs and, finally, attempted suicide.

Then one night a crack in her armor appeared. Alone in her room, for some reason unknown to her, she switched on her television. There Billy Graham was addressing a large crowd in some distant city, but to my friend it seemed he had stepped into her small room and was speaking only to her. What took place after that only God knows, but as she chose to allow His love and light through that tiny crack, the Holy Spirit flooded her heart, and then the entire room, with the glory she knew was Christ.

What confronted my friend that night was beyond her human understanding—and mine. However, we both believe the experience was genuine, for its reality and practical fruit have remained with her ever since. Her life has not been free of trials, nor has she become magically immune to the old temptations. At times, bad choices are still attractive to her. When she reverts periodically to her old self-destructive habits, I am saddened and angry. But God quickly checks my reaction with the reminder that while my temptations are not the same as hers, I have made my own bad choices and have hurt and angered Him, and I am led to ponder these honestly. It is then I see that the whole *direction* of my friend's life has changed, for as a new person in Christ she is in the *process* of being transformed, just as I am still. Temptations will continue to taunt her, but there is a growing steadiness as her submission to Christ allows Him to fight her battles for her.

What a wonderful reminder this friend's life is to me of God's all-encompassing, forgiving love. No matter how many wrong choices we make, creating our own temptations and trials, God never allows *any* of us to wander beyond His reach. If, and when, we shout for His help, help is always at hand as we submit to His unconditional love. God is *always* ready. The choice is *always* ours.

Ask God

If any of you lacks wisdom, he should ask God, who gives generously to all without finding fault, and it will be given to him. But when he asks, he must believe and not doubt, because he who doubts is like a wave of the sea, blown and tossed by the wind. That man should not think he will receive anything from the Lord; he is a double-minded man, unstable in all he does (1:5-7).

James has been telling us that the tests and trials of our lives can be used for our spiritual growth, and for this reason we should count them "pure joy." But how does the strength to turn trials into triumph and the wisdom to make right decisions come to us?

As if anticipating our dilemma James says that if anyone lacks wisdom, he has only to ask God who gives generously. For James, a Christian statesman with a thoroughly Jewish background, wisdom was an unashamedly practical matter. William Barclay describes it this way: "In Christian wisdom there is, of course, knowledge of the deep things of God; but it is essentially practical; it is such knowledge turned into action in the decisions and personal relationships of everyday life" (*The Daily Study Bible,* "The Letters of James and Peter," Revised edition, Westminster Press). It is wisdom that enables us to conduct our lives in a way that honors God. Furthermore, God wants us to ask because He wants to give. Generosity flows forth from His very nature, and it is the spirit in which He gives every gift.

But James continues by telling us to "ask in faith, with no doubts." Like his brother, Jesus, whose teaching was filled with allusions to nature and commonplace sights and experiences, James uses an example familiar to almost anyone then and now. Having lived many years near the ocean's edge in California, I can picture the waves tossing about restlessly, a symbol of my soul's confusion when the result of a wrong choice tosses my faith about like some unpredictable wind. James recognizes that when you and I allow this to happen, we become the *dipsuchos,* meaning, literally, a person with two souls—in this case one believing and the other disbelieving. Inner warfare and confusion are the inevitable and terrible consequences, and I find that my most diligent human strivings are powerless in the face of such instability. But, thank God, we are not meant to depend upon our own meager resources. Our generous, loving God is always at hand, waiting for us to ask for His wisdom and anything else that we need in order to honor Him with our lives. He promises to make a home within us, and that promise provides an absolute assurance for faith—unwavering, steady, and sure.

Standing Through the Struggle
For me, James 1:12 puts the finishing touch on James' theme of trials and the Christian's response. Clearly reminiscent of Jesus, James speaks in the form of a beatitude on the subject:

> Blessed is the man who perseveres under trial, because
> when he has stood the test, he will receive the crown
> of life that God has promised to those who love Him.

The blessing is for the person who "perseveres under

trial," the one who trusts God to use every struggle as a means of growth, and believes God will see him through every conceivable heartache, failure, and trial. The blessing is for those whose joy is not molded by life's happier circumstances, but by the fact that God is with them *through every* circumstance. The blessing is for the person who "endures" temptation, the one who has the perseverance, steadfastness, and patience spoken of in verses 3-4. And this person, having stood the test, will receive a reward that James calls "the crown of life." But endurance is not the sole prerequisite of blessedness; the crown of life is promised to those who endure *and* who love God.

The late Dr. Frank Gaebelein, in his wonderfully concise book on James, *Faith That Lives,* speaks directly to this point:

> It is not just endurance under trial, holding out against temptation, that is singled out for blessedness and reward. After all, there is a sort of stoical patience that keeps on through the most severe testing and yet, admirable as it may be, is far from Christian. The endurance of the Christian is of quite another order; its difference is in respect to love *(Faith That Lives,* Moody Press, p. 41).

Dr. Gaebelein emphasizes that James, very early in his letter, sets apart Christian virtue from any other standard of behavior. And the dividing line between these is love.

But what is this crown promised to those who love and persevere? It is no less than the *crown of life* or, the *crown which consists of life.* Here, James is telling us that the steadfast and loving Christian will not merely survive the ordeals of life in what the poet E.E. Cummings calls an "undead" state; rather, that person will know the joy, the pain, and the richness of living and loving to the very limits of her emotions. She will experience the goodness and fullness of life as God designed it to be.

I can think of no better example of this kind of perseverance than one which is intimately close to my heart. Our

youngest son, Jamie, who has recently authored the book
An Uncommon Gift, was diagnosed as being dyslexic and
hyperkinetic at the age of seven. Dyslexia is a common
learning disability among children and adolescents, especially males, which affects perception and causes messages
received by the eye to be confused by the brain. In this
way, such basic skills as reading, writing, and arithmetic
become tasks of nightmarish proportions (the word *saw*
might be perceived as "was" or a number 6 becomes a "9")
until the brain, through the unrelenting discipline of the
dyslexic, is retrained to translate what it receives properly.
On top of this, hyperactivity only served to aggravate
Jamie's dyslexia since his need to be in constant motion and
his distractability made the necessary discipline painfully
elusive. Far too many dyslexics are crushed psychologically
and intellectually when, for one reason or another, their
disability is not dealt with.

Jamie was a much-loved child. His other weapons against
his learning disability were first, a sense of God in his life—
then gut determination and perseverance—and I mean perseverance with a capital P. In the beginning, his homework
assignments would take him three times as long to complete as most of his classmates; when success wasn't immediate, which it rarely is for the struggling dyslexic, the sting
of ridicule was a familiar wound. For many years the easy
friendships and hours of play which seem the inalienable
rights of all children, had to take a poor second place to
Jamie's need for emotional control and academic discipline.
He was engaged in a battle. He persevered.

By high school he had won—at least on the academic
front. But a frightening inner feeling let Jamie know that all
was not well and that he longed for something deeper.
Jamie had fought so long and hard that relationships had
been pushed to the background, and now he had to learn to
let go of his tight control and love others, to allow himself
to be loved by them and, perhaps most important, to begin
to love himself. Again, God's miraculous love covered Jamie

through this new and turbulent battle. Again, he and God won—and continue to win. But Jamie's own words tell it better than I ever could:

I may always have to confront bits of my LD [Learning Disability] in the years ahead. . . . I must not avoid the pain of struggling with those challenges. It is through facing such pain that I will grow. Those of us with learning disorders must keep in mind that we are fortunate to have been chosen for the privilege of fighting our battles. God would not have given us the disorder if He did not also intend to give us the resources to combat it. Those of us who have such disabilities will see evidence of God's providence and rich grace that "normal" people may not even dream exist. But through our pain we will gain sensitivity, and through our struggle we will be taught discipline, and if there comes a time when we can no longer fight the battle on our own . . . then we will learn one of the greatest lessons of all: Our dependence upon God and upon committed relationships will carry us through. . . .

It's going to take me some time to follow His example, but I can't think of anything better to do with my life. I trust Him, even with my fears and apprehensions. I know now that He will never let me go. At times I offend Him and He reacts in righteous anger. He confronts the wrong that I have done, yet He never stops loving me. At those times when I make Him proud by accepting His will over my own, He commends me— but He makes it very clear that my obedience isn't the reason why He loves me. So it does me no good to argue that I am too dumb to be loved; nor can I claim that any kind of achievement has earned me His love. He simply does love. And that is the way I want to relate. That is the way I want to win the final struggle against a disability that has become—in an amazing sense—a blessing. I really mean that (*An Uncommon Gift*, Westminster Press, pp. 165-166).

Jamie is now a student at Princeton Theological Seminary preparing for the Gospel ministry. God is already using the pain and perseverance of his life to minister to others in their need.

I can never hear Andrae Crouch's song, "Through It All" without thinking of Jamie and feeling very, very grateful.

> I thank God for the mountains,
> And I thank Him for the valleys,
> I thank Him for the storms He brought me through;
> For if I'd never had a problem,
> I wouldn't know that He could solve them,
> I'd never know what faith in God could do.
> (© 1971 by Manna Music, Inc., 2111 Kenmore Ave., Burbank, CA 91504. International copyright secured. All rights reserved. Used by permission.)

> *Our Father,*
> *Thank You that when our troubles confuse and confound us, we can go to You in confidence, asking for help in our times of need.*
>
> *Thank You for Your wisdom which helps us sort out our trials from Your perspective. Thank You too for Your strength which enables us to endure and persevere through our trials and for Your goodness which uses them for growth in our lives.*
>
> *Indeed, "blessed, happy are those who love God as they persevere through trials. They will be given a crown; the promised abundant life, through Jesus Christ our Lord." Amen.*

Do not merely listen to the Word, and so deceive yourselves. Do what it says. Anyone who listens to the Word but does not do what it says is like a man who looks at his face in a mirror and, after looking at himself, goes away and immediately forgets what he looks like. But the man who looks intently into the perfect law that gives freedom, and continues to do this, not forgetting what he has heard, but doing it—he will be blessed in what he does.

If anyone considers himself religious and yet does not keep a tight rein on his tongue, he deceives himself and his religion is worthless. Religion that God our Father accepts as pure and faultless is this: to look after orphans and widows in their distress and to keep oneself from being polluted by the world.

FOUR

TRUE RELIGION: WHERE THE RUBBER MEETS THE ROAD

Spiritual mirror-gazing is a practice most Christians engage in to some extent, though probably few of us are really very accomplished at it. Certainly, no one has mastered the art, that is, the difficult task of perceiving ourselves for what we are in the mirror of God's truth and then allowing the flaws and faults to be smoothed away. To hear the Word and to understand and even profess it are one matter, but to be transformed by it is entirely another. Even the most genuine and well-meaning Christians are guilty of lapses in the application of the Word to everyday life, and the effects can be sadly damaging.

An example comes to my mind which involved a dynamic Christian leader—I'll call her Mrs. Jones—and another woman who had been both a teacher of mine and later a dear friend. The episode took place years ago when my friend was standing in a long line to get a ticket to a live radio program. My friend was never known to mince words, and one of her clearly expressed convictions was that competent adults should carry their own weight in the world. That meant, for one, that they should be accountable to the fundamental rules of courtesy.

You can imagine that my even-handed friend was more

than a little perturbed when she saw a woman rather impe-
riously and rudely cut into the front of the line in which
she had been, quite properly, awaiting her turn. And then
she recognized that woman, who was none other than Mrs.
Jones, the much-admired Christian leader at the large and
prestigious church my friend attended. No words passed
between these two women, but my friend, who at that
point in life was still struggling to go beyond a vague
"churchiness" to a real relationship with God, got a message, and not a very good one. None of us is perfect and
perhaps it was a bit unfair of her to base her opinion on
such a brief encounter, but from then on my friend viewed
Mrs. Jones and her ministry with deep skepticism. Of
course, I was heartsick when I heard her account, for I was
a new Christian and my earnest prayer at that time was that
my friend would join me and experience God's transform-
ing love. Eventually she did, but it was in spite of Mrs.
Jones' lapse in common courtesy. As for Mrs. Jones, she was
never even aware of the impression she made, and I believe
she would have been genuinely repentant if she had been.

There is a lesson here for all of us. As Christians we
cannot be too careful in our efforts to be molded, inwardly
and outwardly, to God's Word. And whether we like it or
not, we *are* being watched.

The Mirror Image

Do not merely listen to the Word, and so deceive
yourselves. Do what it says (v. 22).

James repeats his admonition to live out our faith many
times throughout his letter. It is, in fact, his underlying
theme. For James, *this* is where the rubber meets the road.

In order for us to understand what he means, James uses
a mirror analogy to underscore this unique truth. Those
who hear the Word but never act on it are like people who
look in a mirror, see themselves clearly (the phrase translated literally means, "sees the natural face of their birth"), but
then immediately turn away without acting on what has

been seen.

The purpose of a mirror, of course, is to let us see ourselves with the intent of making needed changes and repairs. When we treat God's Word carelessly, we catch a casual glance of the truth, but we soon forget what we have seen—and that is the end of that. Others of us pass in front of the mirror, stop in our tracks, and get a good, long look, yet we fail to act on what we see. We mistakenly believe that seeing (and hearing) is the same as doing.

Warren Wiersbe wisely counsels:

> If we are to use God's mirror profitably, then we must gaze into it carefully and with serious intent (1:25). No quick glances will do. We must examine our own hearts and lives in the light of God's Word. This requires time, attention, and sincere devotion. . . . After seeing ourselves, we must remember what we are and what God says, and we must *do the Word.* The blessing comes in the doing, not in the reading of the Word (*Be Mature,* Victor Books, pp. 55-56).

It is dangerous to treat the mirror of God's Word carelessly. For when we read and study and begin to see ourselves as we really are and *then,* turn away, pretending not to have seen at all, *that* is risky business. Perhaps Mark Twain was alluding to this issue when he commented, "It is not the Scripture I don't understand that bothers me—it is the Scripture I *do* understand." To see or understand and then to turn away is to ignore the responsibility that accompanies the seeing. A kind of insensitivity and insincerity are the inevitable result, and in James' words we are then merely deceiving ourselves.

A harsh pronouncement? Yes, I thought so too—left to itself. But there is more. Next, James says:

> The man who looks intently into the perfect law that gives freedom, and continues to do this, not forgetting what he has heard, but doing it—he will be blessed in what he does (v. 25).

The verb translated *looks* means to "peer intently" or to

"carefully examine," as if one were looking into a magnifying mirror. And so it is now when any of us looks in God's mirror this way. We see the true picture. And if we follow through and act on what we see, we then become "doers of the Word" and our religion is no longer vain.

Pure Religion

I am a great admirer of James' predictable practicality, and his section on pure religion is one I find wonderfully helpful.

He begins, "If anyone considers himself religious." The word he uses for religious is *threskeia*, and it is used only four times in the New Testament, twice here in James. *Threskeia* means the external, outward expression of religion, including church worship, gatherings and meetings, prayers in public, etc. James is not condemning these expressions of religion as invalid, per se, but he is claiming that they are empty without a life of active commitment. He warns us of the great temptation to allow ritual and decorum to form a substitute for the reality of faith which always includes sacrifice and service.

Frederick Buechner says it so well:

> Phrases like Worship Service or Service of Worship are tautologies. To worship God means to serve Him. Basically there are two ways to do it. One way is to do things for Him that He needs to have done—run errands for Him, carry messages for Him, fight on His side, feed His lambs, and so on. The other way is to do things for Him that you need to do—sing songs for Him, create beautiful things for Him, give things up for Him, tell Him what's on your mind and in your heart, in general rejoice in Him—and make a fool of yourself for Him the way lovers have always made fools of themselves for the one that they love (William Willimon, *The Service of God*).

Worshiping God and serving Him are inseparable Christian activities for Buechner. And their coming together produces genuine religion. Likewise, early on in his letter, James lists some of the ways real religion will be manifested in our lives.

BRIDLING THE TONGUE. "If anyone considers himself religious and yet does not keep a tight rein on his tongue, he deceives himself and his religion is worthless" (v. 26).

Here James speaks to the need of all Christians to submit their speech to God. It must have been as common for people in the early church to claim discipleship one minute, and let their speech betray them the next, as it is today. Apparently, James has in mind the kind of person whose tongue was like an unbridled horse, but we are not told whether this lack of restraint refers to cutting criticism, slander, untruthful statements, or vulgar speech. Perhaps that's really best, for then each one of us can hear his warning and apply it to our own place of need.

Certainly James leaves no doubt that an uncontrolled tongue in any area is a sign that pure religion is not prevailing in our lives. We may go through all the right motions and be convinced that we are religious, yet without producing the pure fruit we are only deceiving ourselves. And when it comes to going through the motions and fooling ourselves, we can be very resourceful.

I remember vividly a night some time ago when Louie and I joined a group of very patriotic, highly respected, upright (religious) leaders for dinner. It was an unusually elegant setting with every outward trapping of sophistication and charm. However, as the evening progressed, the polished veneer wore thin. I was appalled as a surprising number of the guests began cutting down nearly every ethnic and political group outside their own narrow circle. The talk became increasingly oppressive and obscene until finally I became so uncomfortable that I did something very uncharacteristic. Putting down my fork and clearing my throat nervously, I made a dissenting speech. My heart pounded and my voice trembled, but when I was finished I felt better. Better that is, until the Spirit convicted me of going beyond "speaking the truth in love" to being judgmental. It was a question not so much of words, but of attitude, and I found myself repenting.

These were brothers and sisters. We held very different opinions about many things, but that did not have to separate us. To differ openly is healthy; to hold judging attitudes is not. Karl Barth once wrote, "I must repent myself back into the family—back to God." That night sitting at the table, I did just that. And I knew when it was done that the words James spoke regarding the unbridled tongue obstructing the flow of "pure religion" was true of unbridled attitudes as well.

DOING DEEDS OF LOVE. "Religion that God our Father accepts as pure and faultless is this: to look after orphans and widows in their distress" (v. 27).

Now James reminds us that what we profess—what we hear in the quiet places of our souls and in the sanctuaries as we worship—must be lived out in the noisy, hurting places of life. And the example he cites is a simple, everyday deed of love—visiting those who hurt and have needs. The verb he uses, *episkeptesthai*, is the same one used in Matthew 25:36-43 with reference to visiting the sick, and it means more than a nice social call. The implication is to visit the needy with ministry as the goal, with no thought of what can be gotten, but only what can be given.

A friend of ours in the U.S. Senate has shared the weariness he carries because everyone seems to want, need, or expect something from him—favors, jobs, the use of his name, etc. You can understand how touched he was when a minister came to his office and simply asked, "How can I be of service to *you*?" As far as he could remember, this was the first time anyone had ever said that to him without strings attached. True, he was not widowed or orphaned, but he was a lonely leader in need of *episkeptesthai*, a visit with ministry as its goal. How simple our deeds of love can be, yet how essential a part of our religion they are.

LIVING A PURE LIFE. "Religion that God our Father accepts

as pure and faultless is . . . to keep oneself from being polluted by the world" (v. 27).

Here James reminds us that we are not to buy into the world and its ways or be part of what Dr. Frank Gaebelein calls "that Christ-rejecting system that surrounds us."

Similarly, Karl Barth's description of the forces of this world is *das nichtige*, that which says "no" to God. And no place can I find a more graphic picture of such "no-ness" than in Romans 1:28-32:

> And since they did not see fit to acknowledge God, God gave them up to a base mind and to improper conduct. They were filled with all manner of wickedness, evil, covetousness, malice. Full of envy, murder, strife, deceit, malignity, they are gossips, slanderers, haters of God, insolent, haughty, boastful, inventors of evil, disobedient to parents, foolish, faithless, heartless, ruthless. Though they know God's decree that those who do such things deserve to die, they not only do them but approve those who practice them (RSV).

These are some of the evils that make up the "Christ-rejecting system that surrounds us." And though they surround, they are not to overwhelm and consume. We live *in* the world, but it is not to live *in* us.

> Just as a ship must navigate in the ocean while its inside engines, cargo, crew and passengers are kept separate from the ocean, so the Christian, while living in this world, is yet apart from it. When the ocean gets into the ship, it begins to sink; when the world seeps into a Christian life, that life is headed for wreckage (Frank Gaebelein, *Faith That Works*).

Spot-free Living

Standing in front of my washing machine this morning, I was thinking of the significance of living *in* the world, yet not allowing the world to "seep" into our lives. I happened to be sorting laundry, making a separate pile for clothes that needed special attention. Each piece that went into that pile had been spotted by a surprise attack of spaghetti sauce, a dribble of mustard, or a blob of purple grape juice. As the mountain grew, I noticed that the worst stains were on the clothes made of soft, absorbent fabrics. As I worked on them, piece by piece, they jealously held the stains and stubbornly resisted my highly advertised (and overrated) spot-removing spray like the good mess-blotters they were!

In the same wash, I had another pile of clothes that had been worn and needed to be laundry-fresh before being worn again. But these pieces were made of sturdy material that had been chemically treated to repel stains. They had never been pampered, and had had their share of hard use, yet they were beautifully "unspotted" by messy "surprise attacks" and spills.

Of course, all analogies break down at some point and this one is no exception. Yet I smiled and thanked God as I made the connection. He indeed puts us right in the middle of the world where He can use us—and at the same time He provides for us the guiding and protecting power of His Holy Spirit who enables us to resist the spotting and marring of the world upon our lives. In, but not *of.*

Whenever I think of being *in* the world, but not taken over *by* it, I am led to consider the condition of my heart. Surely *heart*-condition is the key to not being "worldly"—or so it is for me. And *that* makes me think of a special friend of ours who I will call Bruce.

Bruce and his wife are long-time covenant friends who have become our brother and sister in the Lord. We've been through a lot together and love each other very much. Recently, when Bruce had a heart flare-up that had all the signs of a real heart attack, we were extremely concerned. Early one morning the phone rang; it was Bruce calling from his hospital room. Louie had already gone to church for a full day of meetings and would not be available until evening, so Bruce began telling *me* how God had been dealing with him as he was forced to lie quietly, hour after hour. Then he asked if I would come to the hospital to pray with him. "And come as fast as you can. It's important," he said.

As I drove the few blocks from our home to the Capitol Hill Hospital, I prayed for our friend—and for myself—for I felt certain he wanted me to pray for his physical healing.

But I was wrong.

When I arrived in Bruce's room, in his characteristically straight-out honest way, he let me know he was not nearly as concerned about his *body* as he was about his spirit. He spoke with great feeling about the way he longed to love God and others the way he once had. And with tears streaming down his face, he confessed how much he needed God to cleanse his life from selfishness.

I was deeply moved by the purity of his desire, and I will never forget his words as we wept together just before I left his room:

> Dear God,
>
> More than a *healed* heart, give me a *clean* heart.

What an impact Bruce made on my life that morning months ago, for it had been a very long time since I had asked God for a clean heart. Now I find myself praying almost daily—and some days *many* times—

> Create in *me* a clean heart, O God; and renew a right
> spirit within me (Ps. 51:10, KJV).

And this is where I have to begin if I am sincere in following James' admonition to live practically for Christ, *in* the world, yet remain true to Him in not becoming worldly myself.

I like the distinctions Dietrich Bonhoeffer makes between a Christian and the world:

> Where the world seeks gain, the Christian will re
> nounce it. Where the world exploits, he will dispossess
> himself, and where the world oppresses, he will stoop
> down and raise up the oppressed. If the world refuses
> justice, the Christian will pursue mercy, and if the
> world takes refuge in lies, he will open his mouth for
> the dumb, and bear testimony to the truth (*The Mar-*

tyred Christian, edited by Joan Winmill Brown, Macmillan, p. 66).

But *in* the world we must be. Or else how can we do those things for God that need to be done? How can we love a world we do not touch?

This is the miracle—that as the love of Christ works through us, the salt of our lives is rubbed into society—and God's light, which we reflect, illumines the darkest and most oppressive corners of the earth.

Yes, *in* the world in the most relevant and practical ways, yet—by His grace—somehow protected and unpolluted by it.

> *Our Father,*
> *Create in us a clean heart and renew a right spirit within us so we can help change the world for You, without allowing the world to change us.*
>
> *Help us to live true to Your teaching in the midst of a society that rewards false values at every turn. May pure religion flow freely from our lives as a natural overflow of our love, worship, and service to You. Amen.*

My brothers and sisters, as believers in our glorious Lord Jesus Christ, don't show favoritism. Suppose a man comes into your meeting wearing a gold ring and fine clothes, and a poor man in shabby clothes also comes in. If you show special attention to the man wearing fine clothes and say, "Here's a good seat for you," but say to the poor man, "You stand there" or "Sit on the floor by my feet," have you not discriminated among yourselves and become judges with evil thoughts?

Listen, my dear brothers and sisters: Has not God chosen those who are poor in the eyes of the world to be rich in faith and to inherit the kingdom He promised those who love Him? But you have insulted the poor. Is it not the rich who are exploiting you? Are they not the ones who are dragging you into court? Are they not the ones who are slandering the noble name of Him to whom you belong? If you really keep the royal law found in Scripture, "Love your neighbor as yourself," you are doing right. But if you show favoritism, you sin and are convicted by the law as lawbreakers. For whoever keeps the whole law and yet stumbles at just one point is guilty of breaking all of it.

FIVE
NO SNOBBERY ALLOWED

James 2:1-10 shows us another of the very practical ways we are to demonstrate our faith in everyday life. In essence, James is saying, "My brothers and sisters, snobbery and faith in our glorious Lord Jesus Christ simply do not mix."

According to the *Expositors Bible Commentary,* the Greek construction of this verse indicates the "forbidding (of) a practice already in progress." Perhaps, then, James' command not to show favoritism would be more precisely translated, "STOP showing favoritism." Indeed, farther on James says, "You *have* insulted the poor" (v. 6), so we know that his readers were already guilty of one form of snobbery. But James not only issues a warning here, he also gives the underlying reason for the unacceptability of favoritism and discrimination. And I *love* what he says, or more accurately, what he doesn't say. He doesn't offer any secondary arguments such as, "It isn't nice to show favoritism" or "People feel put down when they are discriminated against." He simply insists that snobbery is totally incompatible with belief in our glorious Lord. For within the church, the gathering of believers bound together by a "glorious" Creator, external distinctions are to have no bearing on a person's worth.

How well I remember the morning I took an alcoholic friend to a religious meeting where I hoped she would be encouraged in her fragile new commitment to Christ. She was from a very racy (even sordid) background and had come to Christ out of a sense of desperate need.

That morning when I picked her up, she was dressed all in black, and the price tag that dangled from one sleeve of her dress told me she had probably bought it just for this occasion (her first exposure to a group of "churchy women").

Her flamboyant makeup and hairdo, coupled with her fancy low-cut dress, made her look more like a hostess at a casino than a guest at a "Christian huddle" (a term borrowed from Becky Pippert). But behind my friend's outrageous getup there was a truly beautiful and very tender person . . . someone who very much needed the nurture and friendship such a "huddle" could provide. So I took the risk of bringing her into the group as my guest.

But my heart sank as I heard one woman whisper, while watching my friend: I wonder what *she's* doing here? What could she possibly have in common with *us?*"

"How about Jesus Christ?" the woman standing next to her replied with a quiet, firm resolve in her voice.

Fortunately, *she* was a Christian who was "living true" in this matter of not judging people by externals. I will be forever grateful that it was *her generous* attitude and not the exclusiveness of the first woman that prevailed that day. As a result, my friend had a warm and touching welcome into the Christian family—and Christ was honored. *Really,* so much harm can be done when we claim to love God and then dishonor Him by clinging to attitudes that are incompatible with His nature.

The *Expositors Bible* puts it this way: "The stress on Christ as 'glorious' heightens the gross inconsistency of allowing favoritism and discrimination to be associated with faith in such an exalted person as Christ." And to that I shout, "AMEN!"

Catering to the Rich

> Suppose a man comes into your meeting wearing a
> gold ring and fine clothes, and a poor man in shabby
> clothes also comes in. If you show special attention to
> the man wearing fine clothes and say, "Here's a good
> seat for you," but say to the poor man, "You stand
> there" or "Sit on the floor by my feet," have you not
> discriminated among yourselves and become judges
> with evil thoughts? (vv. 2-4)

It's likely that James had seen this sort of thing, or something very close to it actually happening in those first Christian assemblies or he would not have spoken to the issue so
clearly. We can imagine the scene as James witnessed it,
and even sense the anger in his heart. We know historically
that the world into which the Christian church was born
was a place of rigid divisions. The rich were *very* rich, and
the poor *very* poor. The evidence of wealth—lavish robes,
costly jewelry—was flaunted. In fact, some people even
rented rings for those special occasions when they wanted
to make an impression!

In contrast, the poverty of the poor was just as apparent.
It was, of course, one thing for the world to show partiality
in favor of the rich, but when that attitude seeped into the
church, James hit it hard. He stated unequivocally—even
harshly—that exclusivism had no place in the life of a believer. He was angered by snobbery, and so should we be
when we see it rear its ugly head in our churches today.
Our secularity in the way we go about God's business often
far exceeds what is necessary or right. We too, in ways
subtle and obvious, say to the wealthy, "You come sit right
up front please."

Churches and parachurch groups often cater to those
with money, primarily because of their giving potential.
Sadly, the undue time and attention given to a few wealthy
people can detract from the valid needs of others who may
not have the ability to give in the same way. How far that is
from our Lord, who loved and desired to bless the rich

young ruler, but did not chase after him. Neither did He go out after Herod because he was a powerful leader with enormous "giving potential."

Recently, I was visiting friends in another state who are long time Christians and belong to a large and active church in their city. Lila and Jim have a strong personal faith, and are involved in a practical ministry of justice that is making a difference in their community. One afternoon during my visit Lila told me this story.

Three young men who were among their many un-churched friends had apparently taken notice of the way they lived. Jim and Lila's bringing together of faith and works had so impressed these men that they asked them one day, straight out, what made them "so different." Eager-ly, my friends witnessed to the trio about the reality of Christ in their lives and told them about their church. The men accepted an invitation to attend some Sunday. And when they did visit, their reaction to the service was very positive. Each one signed a visitor's card and checked the little box that indicated they wanted a visit from the pastor.

The week passed without a call, which they understood. After all, even *they* knew that pastors have busy schedules. The next Sunday, they were eager to return to the church and once more signed three cards requesting a visit—with the same lack of response. Again, they understood. Pastors were human, and if they *never* got a call from one of them they were still gaining something of value from worship.

The third Sunday they attended they didn't bother filling out the visitor's cards. But one of the three, a man of con-siderable financial means, slipped a check for several hun-dred dollars into the offering plate. And that week, two of the three pastors serving the church contacted the "big giver" personally; one asked him out to lunch to discuss his "spiritual needs." That response the three men *didn't* un-derstand, and disenchanted, they did not return to church the next Sunday, nor have they since.

Needless to say, Jim and Lila felt sick at heart and betrayed. Even now as I think about it, I have the uneasy feeling that this is probably taking place with just slightly varied scenarios in churches all across our country. And I can hear James shouting to us through the centuries, "Brothers and sisters, this ought not to be so!"

Rich in Faith

> Listen . . . has not God chosen those who are poor in the eyes of the world to be rich in faith and to inherit the kingdom He has promised those who love Him? (v. 5)

In terminology again reminiscent of the Beatitudes, James suggests that the poor in the eyes of the world, if they know and follow Christ, are really "rich in faith." As "heirs of the kingdom" with an eternal inheritance, they are not poor in any way that lasts. This doesn't mean, of course, that James is endowing the poor with flawless character, or poverty with inherent goodness. Rather, he points out that any church which holds an exclusive, worldly attitude toward the poor is shortsighted and shallow in its treatment of people and dishonoring to the Lord.

There *is* certainly a poverty that enriches when it puts us in touch with our fundamental human need and spiritual bankruptcy. God honors that kind of poverty. And though it is not impossible, it is without question more difficult for the "rich young rulers" of our world to realize their spiritual needs (Mark 10:17-23).

Paul confirms that the early church was composed primarily of common people: "Not many of you were wise according to worldly standards, not many were powerful, not many were of noble birth" (1 Cor. 1:26, RSV). Therefore, when the early church began to insult the poor and defer to the rich, James just couldn't understand it. He told them it was not only unworthy of their faith in Christ—it didn't make sense!

Exposing this incongruity, James asks three pointed questions:

- Is it not the rich who are exploiting you?
- Are they not the ones who are dragging you into court?
- Are they not the ones who are slandering the noble name of Him to whom you belong? (vv. 6-7)

And James' dispersed flock knew well the answers. For in addition to the very real and visible gap between the "have's" and the "have-not's," there was widespread exploitation of the poor by some of the rich. The poor were desperately impoverished, and moneylenders were ruthless—and everywhere! The interest they charged on borrowed money was so high it amounted to legalized robbery. And if that was not enough, a custom called "summary arrest" allowed the loan sharks to literally snatch their poor debtors off the streets and pull them into court. The poor had no rights against their lenders, and were quite naturally intimidated and fearful. Furthermore, it was these people of corrupted wealth who made light of the name *Christian* and used it in an insulting way.

Certainly we can understand why James saw such a strong link between the possession of wealth and its misuse. Yet he does not absolutely equate the two. Wealth, per se, was not the culprit; rather the wrong user of wealth was the one he was taking to task. But the distinction does not change the message for James' readers. For believers who proudly bear and cherish the name of Jesus to turn around and show partiality to the very ones who blasphemed His holy name is simply not congruent.

Snobbery and Faith Don't Mix

If you really keep the royal law found in Scriptures, "Love your neighbor as yourself," you are doing right. But if you show favoritism, you sin and are convicted by the law as lawbreakers. For whoever keeps the whole law and yet stumbles at just one point is guilty of breaking all of it (vv. 8-10).

Here James returns to the core of his message. Exclusive

attitudes are not worthy of Christ, because they break His "royal law." On the other hand, when we *keep* the "royal law" we do "right" by showing favor to *all* God's people, poor and rich alike. I like that. The "royal law" commands us to love our neighbor as ourselves and not just the poor to the exclusion of the rich. For my neighbors are poor *and* rich, and there are many who fall in between. We are to welcome *all* people, without distinction, in just the same way we would hope to be welcomed ourselves.

Why? Because people are of equal inherent value in the eyes of God regardless of their wealth or their lack of it. When we love a rich person, it should be for her as an individual—not for her money. Nor should rich people be deferred to above others. But if we *do* defer, James calls it what it is—an expression of sin in our lives. Conversely, when we love all people *without* respect to their station in life, it is an expression of Christ's love.

As I put aside these verses on exclusive attitudes and close my commentaries for the moment, I must pause and let these strong words take root in my heart. I am stirred as I realize what a difference the Gospel of Jesus Christ will make in our lives when we allow Him to be Lord and take His royal law seriously. It troubles me that so many in our day treat exclusiveness as a slight offense—a half respectable and permissible social error that we tend to wink at.

As we have seen, James' perception is not so casual. If, as he says, unjust favoritism is a sin against the very heart of the Lord, that is *serious* business. And there are so many ways we can fall into acting with favoritism. The Jews to whom James was writing exhibited exclusiveness not only in their attitudes toward the poor, but also in their racial prejudices against the Samaritans, their views on women, and their political bias against the Romans. (To be resistant to the oppressive Roman system was one thing, but as Christians, to be found hating the Romans as people was quite another!) These are the glaring examples, and there were undoubtedly others that were more subtle, but equally hurtful. And we today can see ourselves in similar situations. Our racial bigotry has taken an enormous toll in this century, all the way from the ovens of Auschwitz to the streets of our own cities during the civil rights struggles of the 1960s. And, sadly, it isn't over yet.

Women are still struggling to be "all they're meant to be," and much more so in some other parts of the world than here in the U.S. But there are still some states in our beloved land that deny certain rights to women and make it difficult for women to achieve. While I am eternally grateful to be a woman in this nation and feel a tremendous sense of fulfillment as a woman in Christ, I know of sisters who do not feel the same fulfillment because God has given them gifts they are not yet totally free to use. Until *every one* is free to pursue his or her destiny, under God, I will work and pray for that day—if not for myself, on behalf of others.

And what about the political bias the Jews had against the Romans? Don't we have our own versions of that today? During World War II we were cleverly brainwashed to hate the Germans, then the Japanese, the Russians, the Chinese, and now again the Russians. Surely, as Christians, we must learn to distinguish between evil systems of government and people . . . and not take part in the world's exclusive games. Christ calls us to love *all* people, and our allegiance to Him is above every other.

If we take our discipleship and the teaching of James seriously, we will examine every aspect of our lives, and that will not be an easy task. For within every one of us there resides, *some* place, a tendency toward snobbery. This might manifest itself in the ways we have mentioned, or in other more subtle ways—social relationships, educational stuffiness, pompous attitudes regarding position and prestige. On the other hand, we may be "too religious" to indulge in any of these forms of snobbery, yet we may still fall headlong into exclusivism by not being sensitive to the traps especially laid for our types.

An example that comes to mind is what I would call the

super-denominationalist syndrome. I am a Presbyterian, and happy to be one, but here and there I come across a person who is *so* Presbyterian—or Baptist or Mennonite or whatever—that they look askance at any group or program that doesn't have the stamp of their denomination on it. I am also reminded of an anti-*any* denomination religious community, alarmingly narrow in its exclusivism, for whom membership in the group seems to mean more than being a Christian.

Of course, Christians are not called to accept all practices and embrace all doctrines. We don't have to be wishy-washy about what *we* believe, to be open to other people and what *they* believe. Far from it! But a judgmental narrow-mindedness is too often the mark of religious conviction. We can be downright "uppity" when the Gospel is presented in a way other than our own.

Louie and I have a minister friend from another city who shared his particular brand of snobbery with us in a disarming way. Paul and his wife minister in a large metropolitan area known for its mix of people from every kind of background. Paul and his wife love this diversity, but there was one person in the city who was so "far-out" he really bugged Paul. This man was what Paul considered a "religious nut," and as a minister Paul resented the bad impression he thought this man made for the Gospel. The man dressed bizarrely and was unkempt, and the finishing touch to his unconventional appearance was a gaudy sandwich board plastered with Bible verses and religious slogans which he always wore. Every time Paul saw the man walking the streets of their city, he flinched and looked the other way. Paul would even cross the street to avoid seeing him close-up.

Then something happened in our friend's life that changed many of his attitudes. Through a personal need, Paul had reached out to the One he had loved and served so long, and God responded in a way that left Paul newly open to the Holy Spirit and filled to overflowing with love.

Needless to say, the experience had practical consequences. The next time Paul went into the city on business, he parked his car in an underground parking center and began the short walk down the busy street to the place of his appointment. As he looked up, who did he see coming toward him but the source of his previous hostility and embarrassment—the sandwich-board man. Expecting his familiar hostililty to return, Paul thought, *There's not enough time to cross the street; I'll just look the other way again.* But for some reason, he couldn't. As they drew closer to one another, their eyes met for the first time, and in that gaze Paul realized how much God had changed him from the inside out. Instead of hostility and repulsion, there was love in his heart for this man—a love so unique, God *had* to be its source. And not only love, but a realization of brotherhood because they both belonged to the same Father. No words were exchanged as they passed, but their eyes spoke volumes—acceptance, understanding, and that unique love. So much so, in fact, that Paul stopped in his tracks and turned fondly to watch his new brother until he disappeared into the crowd. It was then he saw for the first time what was written on the back of the sandwich board: THIS IS CLYDE'S WAY OF WITNESSING—WHAT'S YOURS?

As Paul finished sharing this vignette from his spiritual journey with us, I thanked God that indeed *He* is no respecter of persons, and when He is alive and well in our lives, neither are we! Now James' words ring even more clearly in my ears: "Don't ever attempt to combine snobbery (of any kind!) with faith in our glorious Lord Jesus Christ!"

A Snob about Snobs

Though James was one of its strongest advocates, this teaching on favoritism did not originate with him. As a good Jew, James knew the Scriptures well, and they had always spoken with clarity on the subject. As far back as Malachi, we read that God was troubled because the people were not living the way He had instructed them to, and a critical lapse of obedience centered on showing partiality in their judgments (Mal. 2:9). Leviticus 19:15 likewise commands: "You shall do no injustice in judgment. You shall not be partial to the poor or defer to the great, but in righteousness shall you defer to your neighbor." And Ecclesiastes 35:12: "The Lord is judge and with Him is not respect of persons." "The rich and poor meet together; the Lord is maker of them all" (Prov. 22:2, KJV). The totality of Scripture confirms the fact that God is fair and impartial.

What remains then, is for each of us to take an honest look into our hearts and recognize any tendency toward exclusiveness we might harbor, and then offer that disobedience to God. I don't know what it is that you must relinquish, but I am well aware of my own place of struggle.

Recently I was reminded that God still has work to do in this area of my life. It was New Year's Eve. The church was closed and Louie and I were enjoying a rare day at our desks, hoping to clear away some of the debris and get a fresh start on the new year. The phone rang. It was Dan, our eldest son, calling from Washington State where he had flown from Washington, D.C. to do some work for his congressman. Dan is an exceptional young man, a thoughtful, caring Christian who puts his faith to work in everyday life. One ministry he has chosen is volunteer work in a downtown shelter for homeless men. Every Saturday night during the winter months, Dan is responsible to either be at the shelter himself, or to make sure others are there. It is a ministry of presence.

The previous Saturday, Christmas Eve, Dan and our son-in-law Craig had spent the night at the shelter. Knowing he would be out of town the next week, Dan had arranged for two other friends to be there New Year's Eve. But his well-made plans fell through, and some 3,000 miles away Dan was responsible to make alternate arrangements. At a loss at such a distance, he called me with an urgent "HELP," claiming "it was being raised by a 'crusader' mom that got me into this." With a sinking feeling, I thought of the difficulty I would have on the afternoon of New Year's Eve finding people home, free, and willing to spend the night in an abandoned government building filled with homeless people. But Washington was experiencing record cold and I couldn't bear the thought of the shelter closing its doors.

So with a prayer, I dove in and began dialing—and I dialed, and dialed, and *dialed.* Soon I was convinced that everyone I knew was out of town for the holidays. The idea struck me that perhaps a good disguise would enable me to pass for a man. Then Louie and I could do the duty together, and certainly that would be better than making more phone calls! When I suggested the disguise to Louie, he was skeptical about the feasibility of my scheme and told me so by laughing and exclaiming, "No way!"

I kept dialing—and finally, after a *very* long time, I found several people home. To my disappointment, however, the responses I got were less than enthusiastic; I began to detect undertones of exclusivism—politely expressed, but present nonetheless. Be that as it may, the real issue for me at the time was not what I thought *other* people were feeling, but with what I *knew* I was. You see, Dan was right about me. I *am* a "crusader" and there are certain occupational hazards that go along with championing causes. Ironically perhaps, one is the tendency to look *down* on people who look *down* on people—to be a snob about snobs. As I move forward in faith toward maturity, I realize that this too is a kind of partiality God wants to purge from my life.

In spite of my own inverted snobbery which made me feel devastated (and judging) when I sensed exclusive attitudes coming from the other end of the line, I kept making calls until I got a promising lead. A friend of ours put me in touch with a group of young men who live together in a Christian community, and though most of them had gone home for the Christmas holidays, there were three left. Amazingly, they were not only "willing," they were delighted to be asked to spend their New Year's Eve at the shelter.

They had been looking for some practical way to serve in the city, and if this worked well, they would even like their names put on Dan's list as regular recruits.

I had hit the jackpot! I hung up the phone and literally shouted my thanks to God! He had beautifully resolved the immediate dilemma, and just as significantly, He had revealed a weakness I needed to work on. I recognized my former rationalizations about my own brand of snobbery as flimsy excuses, and saw the model of Jesus, open and available as He is to *all* people, taking on a fresh reality! He sees people as they *can* be even more than as they are, and that simple, radical notion holds a great challenge for me.

- Just as Jesus is no respecter of persons, as He is comfortable with the rich or the poor, so I want to be.
- Just as Jesus does not judge people in or out of His fellowship for *any* reason but looks to the inner person and their potential, so I want to do.

Jesus, my Lord, the great equalizer who opens the door to every conceivable type of person, invites them into full fellowship in His kingdom by way of the Cross.

If Jesus opens the door, how dare I close it
    to anyone
    for any reason
by my attitude of snobbery, inverted or otherwise—for this is sin.

Our Father,
Go to the root of our problems. Rid us of the pride,
the selfishness, the insecurity—whatever it is that
causes us to own exclusive attitudes about anyone.
Help us in our journey toward maturity as we
grow up into the person You designed us to be.
Make us like You, Lord.
No respecter of persons—and a lover of all. Amen.

Has not God chosen those who are poor in the eyes of the world to be rich in faith and to inherit the kingdom He promised to those who love Him? Now listen, you rich people, weep and wail because of the misery that is coming upon you. Your wealth has rotted, and moths have eaten your clothes. Your gold and silver are corroded. Their corrosion will testify against you and eat your flesh like fire. You have hoarded wealth in the last days. Look! The wages you failed to pay the workmen who mowed your fields are crying out against you. The cries of the harvesters have reached the ears of the Lord Almighty. You have lived on earth in luxury and self-indulgence. You have fattened yourselves in the day of slaughter. You have condemned and murdered innocent men, who were not opposing you.

SIX

POSSESSED BY POSSESSIONS
OR STEWARDS OF GOD?

Here James affirms the truth that human richness lies in a person's relationship with God and with others. God *always* identifies with the poor. The biblical evidence of this fact is astonishing. All through the Old Testament God's concern for justice and His identification with the poor, the hungry, and the oppressed is a recurring theme. In Proverbs we read that the person "who mocks the poor shows contempt for their Maker" (Prov. 17:5).

When the fullness of time arrived and God came to earth in human form, He chose a young woman from a poor family to bear the Baby Jesus. She and her husband provided a humble birth and a humble home for the child who was God. And they did this in obedience to God their Father, for this was His choice for His only begotten Son, another way of identifying with the poor and lowly of the world.

When Jesus, grown to manhood, delivered His first sermon He said, "He has anointed Me to preach Good News to the *poor*" (Luke 4:18), making it clear that the Gospel would always have a special message for the needy. In the Sermon on the Mount He taught that the "poor in spirit," those who are in touch with their own need, are the people

God can bless. When we look to ourselves, *our* wealth, *our* power, anything or anyone other than God for our security, we are not "poor in spirit."

From His encounter with the rich young ruler (Mark 10:17-27) we learn even more about the pitfalls of wealth. In the words of William Barclay: "It was the simple fact that the Gospel offered so much to the poor and demanded so much from the rich, that it was the poor who were swept into the church. It was, in fact, the common people who heard Jesus gladly, and the rich young ruler who went sorrowfully away because he had "great possessions."

Dependence on God

As I ponder the fact of God's identification with the poor, I must not let myself fall into the trap of inverted snobbery—thinking that God is not concerned with the rich and powerful. He is, of course, or He wouldn't be God. The biblical word is that the kingdom is for *all* people—rich and poor alike. Wealth, in itself, is not wrong. It is not money, but the LOVE and MISUSE of money that do us in (1 Tim. 6:10).

> Money
> Dug from the mountainside,
> Washed in the glen,
> Servant am I,
> Or the *master* of men?
> Earn me, I bless you,
> Steal me, I curse you.
> Hold me and grasp me,
> A fiend *will* possess you.
> Lie for me, die for me,
> Covet me, take me....
> Angel or devil
> I *am* what you make me.
> AUTHOR UNKNOWN

All poor people are not automatically rich in faith. Some

of us tend to romanticize poverty, just as some of us roman-ticize wealth. The truth is, *real* poverty is an indignity. It is often ugly, smelly, and as Dorothy Day put it, a "precarity," a "mitigated or unmitigated captivity to circumstances." But when faith is present *in* poverty, that very precariousness can be a gift. Stripped down to essentials, dependence on God becomes what it should be—a way of life.

But for the wealthy person who also has faith, the road is more difficult. In his book, *Money and Power,* Jacques Ellul rejects the idea of society, whether communist, or capital-ist, or anything in between as the answer to the dilemma of how money and resources are used. He argues for individ-ual responsibility, saying for the Christian, money is not neutral—to be used as we like—but powerful, and to be used in godly ways. Throughout his book Ellul challenges believers to live by the law of grace and not the law of the marketplace (*Money and Power,* InterVarsity Press, 1984). Rich or poor, we all have to deal with the problem of money. But Scripture teaches, and life confirms, that wealthy persons have the potential for greater struggle as they enter the kingdom of God. Their riches make it harder for them to see their own poverty and be in touch with their spiritual needs. And so the essential factors of trust and dependence can slip subtly out of their lives.

But that doesn't *have* to be. Louie and I know earnest believers who do not consider what they have to be their own. They manage assets for the Lord, that is all. We need more North American Christians who have this concept of total stewardship. But I don't want to overlook those I know to be living this way right now. In fact, Louie and I have a friend whose full-time ministry is helping Christians grow in this area of compassion and stewardship. Don McClanen has what is called a *Ministry of Money* and he and his wife, Gloria, take people on pilgrimages to areas of need where they are truly exposed to a suffering world. They hear the sighs and groans of the people, and see with their own eyes the disparity that exists between God's children who have and those who have not. These trips change lives and life-styles, and in my opinion, are making a difference in our world (Don McClanen, *Ministry of Money,* Germantown, Md. 20874).

Mary Hillis has recently returned from one of these tours and has given me permission to share a part of her journal from that trip:

> The pilgrimage . . . was a process of inner and outer vulnerability that has broken me open as never before experienced. Almost from the start I was sick, and there were times when I wondered if I'd be able to continue. The daily weakness, the not knowing, and the pain started the breaking open. I was not able to come from my usual high energy, confidence, and strength.
>
> Then being present in an intimate way to the poorest of the poor, however briefly, completed the process. I am grateful for the breaking open (indeed I know now that is why I went on the pilgrimage) for it has made me grow as nothing else could. . . . The changes wrought, the growth of consciousness, the enlarged perception were mediated by "the least of persons," and I know it was God-in-them who touched me. . . .
>
> The process enabled me to go into my darkness, my fears, so that now I know more of myself. It has sufficiently prepared me to begin making some radical changes in my lifestyle, all in the direction of simplicity. It has given me insight into how I've participated in Third World exploitation and oppression. It has helped me to see that the diseases of the Third World (the diseases of poverty)—starvation, malnutrition, leprosy, prolapsed uteruses—are related to the diseases of the First World (the diseases of affluence)—hypertension, cancer, coronaries, alienation, loneliness; and that this relationship is of critical importance in the struggle for world peace. Henry Okullu, the Angli-

can bishop of Kenya, says that there will be no peace while millions in Africa die of hunger, and millions in North American die of overeating, and tons of food are fed to dogs.

The process has left me with many questions and almost no answers; the issues are complex, and as Mother Teresa says, do not lend themselves to simple problem-solving. Certainly consciousness everywhere has to change for both First World and Third World (and Second World!) inhabitants to move toward fullness of life. The process has helped me to see better my own arrogance and self-righteousness, which are the subtle and mostly hidden result of almost always having a grasp on things. There was no way, sick and experiencing the culture shock of Calcutta, that I could have a grasp on anything.

I saw the joy and peace and centeredness of some saints who have committed their lives to being present to the poorest of the poor. . . . I beheld the spirit, courage, resourcefulness, and strength of the African woman, and I am in awe of her. She is another source of hope for our world. I know now that the poor are among my teachers, and I know through others and my own experience what St. Paul knew—that in weakness there is strength and that God's power is at its best in weakness (2 Cor. 12:9).

The following lines which flowed out of me, unbidden and unedited, after three weeks of pilgrimage and three days in Calcutta probably say best what was happening within:

O Calcutta, what do you have to say to us?
You shock us and shake us out of our comfortableness,
    our circle of isolation.
Your stench, your noise, your homelessness
Is not all outside, it's inside us too
Only we keep it hidden, while you are out in the open.

How can you offer your smile, your life,
Your deep soul eyes that love and do not condemn?
What spirit animates you, inhabits you
That you are not vacant, ground down, and despairing?
What do you know that we do not know?
What riches do you possess that are lost to us?
Do we have the wrong dream?
The dream of things, and ease, and places in the sun,
Stuffing and possessing and accumulating
Until like the vultures we are too laden down to fly,
Too blinded to see what our way of life is doing to
    others and to us.
O Calcutta, I weep over your sons and daughters
Or am I really weeping over myself
My fragile, moist, soft soul center
That has become encrusted with the grime of
    unconsciousness?

    My hope and prayer is for the world to be truly one, a balance of strength and weakness, wealth and poverty, light and dark so that the peace of the running wave, the flowing air, the shining star, the quiet earth, and above all, the peace of the Son of Peace might be with us all. Amen (*The Process of a Pilgrimage*, by Mary Hillis, 12/9/83).

Where True Wealth Is

When James says that the believer who is poor is only so "in the eyes of the world," I wonder if he is suggesting that that person, in the truest sense, is not poor at all? Not that he is denying the reality and pain of physical poverty. I don't think that for a moment. James was far too honest and practical for that. But I do think he was affirming the priority of spiritual riches when he said a poor believer can be rich in faith. He is also affirming that God has chosen the poor for special blessings—as their dependence on God paves the way for eternal riches.

Melville Watson, an Australian barrister and minister, writes movingly of some of the "wealthy poor" he befriended on a recent trip to Africa and the impact they had on his life:

At about 4 P.M. I walked through the slums of the Mathare Valley, one of the worst in Africa. There were families living, eating, loving, and sleeping in humpies of tin, wood, and cardboard no bigger than a large packing case. I picked my way through the maze of deprivation to a hut where three of the Taize brothers live their life of "presence" within the slum.

I knocked on the door and entered. My apprehension vanished in a moment as about a dozen children emerged in half light and started leaping up in the air. They were all over me and, in a moment of spontaneous childishness, I too jumped up and down and shouted, with kids clinging to arms and legs and whatever else they could grab. It was a welcome like none I have known before, and never likely to know again.

After about an hour of holding and stroking kids of all kinds, Brother Dennis took me to meet some of the people of the slum. "Deneece," as they call him, has been there for 5 years and the relationships which this tall, warm Frenchman has established are so deep as to be in the realm of mystery. As people responded to him, and he to them, I had that eerie feeling of what it must have been like to walk with Christ in Palestine.

We returned to the hut where we engaged in a sing song amongst 20 or so raucous kids. The rhythm from the drum was so easy to pick up so I joined in the singing, making up my own words, and holding a warm, wet, retarded child in my lap. It was a delightful experience, but nothing compared with what was to come. . . . .

Then came the moment which to my dying day I will never forget. There came from the side of the room the quiet, clear voice of Dennis: "We pray for the people of Australia, for Ned and his family," and from the group came an equally clear and quiet response, "Jesus, remember them when You come into Your kingdom." It was a moment of wonder, of grace, and overwhelming emotion. In the middle of Africa, a group of slum kids, in a reverence and earnestness previously unexperienced by me, were holding up before God the people of Australia and asking: "Jesus, remember them when You come into Your kingdom."

I thought of Australia luxuriating on its bed of pleasure, stupefied in the euphoria of the Americas Cup, and completely oblivious of the existence of the Mathare Valley slums. The incongruity of it all came down on me like a ton of bricks and I thought to myself: *God, if Australia has any hope at all, it will be because of kids like this.*

On the evening of the 19th of October 1983, a cry from the rejected and deprived one on the cross next to that of Christ rang around the world. God in heaven heard it and, in mercy, looked at Australia and decided to give it, and me another chance of responding to His love.

I am grateful to both Mary and Melville for sharing their heart responses to this new and sensitizing exposure in their lives. I covet their experiences for more "first world" Christians.

Perhaps the bottom line for this section should be: All Christians, rich and poor—first world and third—must know that in themselves they are spiritually bankrupt. It is *only* in our relationship with Christ that true wealth resides.

Wealth That Is Impoverished

Now listen, you rich people, weep and wail because of the misery that is coming upon you. Your wealth has rotted, and moths have eaten your clothes. Your gold and silver are corroded. Their corrosion will testify against you and eat your flesh like fire. You have hoarded wealth in the last days. Look! The wages you failed to pay the workmen who mowed your fields are crying out against you. The cries of the harvesters have reached the ears of the Lord Almighty. You have lived on earth in luxury and self-indulgence. You have fattened yourselves in the day of slaughter. You have condemned and murdered innocent men, who were not opposing you (James 5:1-6).

This is a *tough* passage. It bristles with indignation as James lashes out against unconverted wealth. Following his brother Jesus, James is a powerful advocate for social justice; he warns us about allowing money to become the master instead of the servant. If we make that mistake, we will open the door to all kinds of oppression and exploitation of people and it is *this* that James is denouncing. He must have seen it happening around him in the world in which the early church existed. And from time to time he must have grieved to see the world's ways seep into the church, causing Christians to exploit one another—the rich over the poor—just like those outside of Christ were doing. And his words must have stung those early believers just as they sting me today.

And how can it be otherwise when I am part of a world where 6 percent of the population (my part) consumes approximately one third of the world's wealth, where starvation and malnutrition are endemic, and where this year, in Africa alone, the U.N. predicts 5 million children will die of hunger. As a Christian I can no longer rationalize those statistics away, or spiritualize them. I will pray, but I must not stop there. My prayers must lead me to some kind of action that balances out more equitably the "more than enough" I have with the "less than enough" of others.

If James were to add a postscript to his letter for our day, I believe it would be in the form of a question. In fact, I can almost hear him yell: *Do you or do you not consume more than your share?* And I would have to answer, "I do."

I pray, not only for myself but for all Christians in our great but spiritually needy nation, that we will learn to live more simply and compassionately for others. We could share so much more of what we have, and still have enough.

Some of us may feel God urging us into compassionate living with one great leap, or for others of us God may lead us toward a lean and loving lifestyle by stripping away our possessiveness piece by piece. But either way it *needs* to happen. And it needs to begin *now.*

I remember a young couple we knew years ago in a very affluent part of California. They were newly married, and totally caught up in building their dream house when we met them. Since they were people of enormous means, it was going to be some dream house—not your "white cottage with picket fence to match" variety. As we watched their house grow, we saw their relationship deteriorate. Every decision was a battle, and the "dream house" literally became a monster between them. By the time their house was finished, so was their marriage. They only lived in it together for a few short months before the husband moved out leaving the wife alone in a gorgeous, lonely house. It was so sad. And a lesson that was not wasted on me.

I remember visiting the wife after her husband left, and coming home to our frame house where our three children shared a bedroom, and our baby's crib was in our master bath. That afternoon it looked especially beautiful to me. I was deeply grateful for what we had, but even more for the life-dreams the Lord had given to Louie and to me that had nothing to do with "things."

Henry David Thoreau said, "The possibilities of life diminish as so-called 'means' increase. The best thing a rich man can do to preserve his humanity is to realize the dreams he cherished when he was poor."

James continues his denunciation of oppressive wealth in verses 4-5 of chapter 5. Frank Gaebelein gives a vivid paraphrase of these verses in *Faith That Lives*:

Look out. This starvation of the workers in your fields,
whom you have cheated cry aloud your injustice; the
complaint of the laborers you have been exploiting has
reached the ears of the Lord of hosts Himself. You
have been indulging yourselves by living in the lap of
luxury; but your very self-indulgence is preparing your
wicked hearts for judgment as cattle are fattened for
slaughter.

It's hard to believe James wrote those words for another
age and another culture. They fit our own so well. It is a
message we in the U.S. need to take to heart in the way we
treat others.

I have a new friend who has recently come to the U.S.
from a small troubled nation. She is a lovely woman overflowing with gratitude just to be here where she can work
and worship as she chooses. And she does both well! I don't
think I've ever known a person more willing and eager to
take on tough jobs. But when she first arrived in our country she was desperate for work just to keep food on the
table. An "enterprising" couple, sensing her vulnerability,
hired her. She worked 12 to 14 hours a day for them for
pay far below the minimum wage. They kept her coming
back by withholding what they owed her, until she felt like
a prisoner in their grasp. It was a terrible introduction to
life in the United States—*until* some Christians befriended
her and took an active interest in her welfare. They found
work for her where the pay was equitable, and urged her to
leave the situation where she was being cheated daily. Her
cries of injustice had "reached the ears of the Lord of hosts
Himself" and He found some people who would stand with
Him on behalf of a neglected woman.

But I remember another time when Christians did not
come off so well. After the birth of one of our children, I
went through a time of physical weakness where I needed
some part-time help for a while. I called a minister's wife
who I knew had someone help her one day a week to ask
if the woman who worked for her would have time to come

to me occasionally. It turned out that she could, and she did. It was a wonderful answer for me—until I received an irate call from the minister's wife railing at me for "ruining a good deal" for her by paying the woman more than she did. I had inquired about the fair going rate—and had to tell my friend on the other end of the line that that was what I was going to continue paying. To this day I believe she is still angry with me for that.

Strange, isn't it? That woman was a good Christian in many ways, very vocal about her faith, but she failed to see the correlation between her words, and the way she treated an employee who worked for her. What a reminder to each of us to watch for areas of inconsistency in our own lives. We all have blind spots and we need to be open to correction and change. Yes, the scathing warning James gave the early church, "Your very self-indulgence is preparing your wicked hearts for judgment" is a message we need to hear as well!

And what is the answer we must pursue? It is a radical discipleship that will result in a submission of all we are, and all we possess—*including* our money—to Jesus Christ, Lord of our lives. I get so excited as I consider this kind of stewardship and what it could mean in our world. Oh, the people who would be drawn to Christ as they see Christians living obediently and sacrificially! Think of the hunger, pain, and suffering that would be alleviated if we would take seriously Jesus' command to serve Him by serving "the least of these."

In his tough teaching James was not speaking against all wealth, per se; as we have stressed earlier on, he was speaking about the *abuse* of wealth. Frank Gaebelein said, "Properly used, great wealth can be a means of blessing; in consecrated hands, it can be employed for the upbuilding of the work of God."

How true! God needs stewards He can trust with that kind of wealth, people who will share with others not out of guilt, or to exact some self-gratifying response, but simply in obedience and gratitude to their Lord.

Louie and I know a number of such radical stewards, but let me tell you about just one of the couples. Janet and Ned (not their real names) had been married for over 30 years, having both made solid commitments to Christ as youths. They had always been credible Christians, bringing together a rich combination of faith and living. Though not wealthy, they had enough money to live on and some to spare. In fact, they lived simply so they would always have something "spare" to share with others. Their lives were full, and that fullness increased almost as miraculously as the loaves and fishes as they were given for others.

One day Janet said to me in a rather off-handed way, "Ned and I have just come into a lot of money." When I responded casually, she underscored what she had said by adding, "Coke, I mean a *bundle.*" And she wasn't kidding. The result of Ned's good stewardship had made them wealthy people.

I like to think that God had been watching Janet and Ned and knew He could trust their stewardship. They had been faithful over little and so He gave them the opportunity to be faithful over much. His trust was not misplaced. Ned and Janet decided their lives were full as they were. They were pleased with their 2 bedroom apartment, their one car, their relatively simple style of life. They had enough and, for them, enough was enough. They felt that God had other things for them to do with their "over and above" money. So they formed a foundation and began looking for those "other things."

I can't tell you what joy and ministry they are spreading in the name of Christ, and they would be the first to say the joy is *theirs* as they serve the kingdom in this way. Not that their road is easy. That kind of wealth is a heavy responsibility, and they know they are walking a fine line. I have the feeling they are always asking, *What are we doing with the wealth over which God has made us stewards—and what is it doing to us?*

Jacques Ellul writes, "God in Jesus Christ calls the Christian to live according to God's will—in other words, to accomplish something truly extraordinary" (*Money and Power*). Janet and Ned are doing just that! Without a tinge of reservation, I can say they are people whose pocketbooks are just as converted as they are, and that *is* extraordinary! Someone has said, "The chronicle of God's saints is the story of their ever slipping grasp on the things of this world." Janet and Ned wear their worldly possessions very loosely indeed, perhaps because they really believe everything they have—and are—is God's.

As we grow in radical discipleship, that grasp *will* slip for us as well. We too will wear our possessions loosely and become the lovers and sharers God means for us to be.

It's really not a question of money; it is discipleship. The question is: *Are we sincere in wanting to follow Jesus?*

One of our covenant brothers in Washington is a man who, without a doubt, is sincere in pursuing real discipleship. Bill Brehm has written a song that sums it all up for me. I can think of no better way to close this chapter than to share with you the words of his beautiful song, "Ev'rything."

> What will it cost me
>   to follow the Lord?
> What is the cost
>   of a life that's restored?
> If I am willing to walk in His way
> What is the price I must pay?
> Everything, everything—All that I am—
> Everything, everything—All that I have—
> Everything, everything—All that I love
> That is the price I must pay
> That is the price I *will* pay.

Our Father,
Help us understand kingdom economics . . . that when we yield our lives to You, we give up our rights of ownership to everything. Our worldly possessions become instruments of ministry at Your disposal. We cannot possess the people we love—or even our own lives—for You have bought us at a very costly price.

Free us from our human need to possess, and establish us as good and faithful stewards of Your kingdom. Amen.

What good is it, my brothers and sisters, if a man claims to have faith but has no deeds? Can such faith save him? . . . Faith by itself, if it is not accompanied by action, is dead. But someone will say, "You have faith; I have deeds." Show me your faith without deeds, and I will show you my faith by what I do. . . . A person is justified by what he does and not by faith alone. As the body without the spirit is dead, so faith without deeds is dead.

SEVEN

FAITH & WORKS: NOT EITHER/OR, BUT BOTH!

A year ago, Mildred Ellis, a senior citizen and a very loved member of our church, was walking home alone after giving piano lessons at another church nearby. Suddenly, Mildred was forcefully pushed from behind and she fell to the ground, not knowing what had happened and not seeing the three young men who had assaulted her. They took her purse and ran, leaving Mildred bleeding and unconscious on the sidewalk.

That night during a service at church, word reached us that Mildred had been mugged. I slipped away from the meeting and phoned Washington Hospital Center where Mildred had returned to consciousness just minutes before. Her first words to me were, "Colleen, let's pray for those boys. I want them to get help. There's no way I can be a Christian and hold hate in my heart for them." Nothing feigned or calculated here. This was Mildred's heart's response, the reflexive reaction of true faith.

In the days that followed, Mildred remained under the watchful eye of her doctor. Finally, when she was pronounced well, I went with her to court the day she gave her deposition to the prosecuting attorney. His astonishment over her forgiving attitude and her desire to find help for those who had assaulted her had been obvious. Two of the boys confessed, and Mildred chose to be involved in two separate mediation sessions with them. Eventually they entered a court-sponsored program of restitution, and while Mildred is legally kept from knowing their present situations, she has never stopped praying for them. As the prosecuting attorney said when he had finished his questioning, "She's *some* lady!" And she is—some *Christian* lady who doesn't know the meaning of compromise when it comes to putting her faith into practice.

Faith and Works

> For just as the body without the spirit is dead, so faith
> without works is dead (James 2:26).

This is the heart of James' message, or so it is for me. With these strong words, James lays the foundation for his entire letter as he stresses the profound importance of putting spiritual truth into practice. James spells out how this can be done in everyday life, but it is verse 14 which forms the core of these directives:

> What good is it, my brothers, if a man claims to have
> faith but has no deeds? Can such faith save him? Faith
> by itself, if it is not accompanied by action, is dead.

It is precisely this central passage which so many have misunderstood, making James the object of often stinging criticism throughout the centuries. The disagreement focuses on a supposed conflict between James and the Apostle Paul. Martin Luther denounced James' epistle as the "book of straw," for in Luther's understanding it perverted the pure Pauline emphasis on justification by faith alone. And certainly, taken out of the context of the whole book, James 2:14 might be construed as a distortion of the Gospel's message of justification solely by faith.

But James is not talking theology here, he's talking life. The church, then as now, must have been inclined to neglect the essential linking of faith *with* works. Furthermore, James wrote his epistle in A.D. 45—before Paul had written any of his letters, so he could not have been influenced by Paul's thoughts. This is not to suggest that a major disagreement *would* have arisen between James and Paul had they been writing at the same time, for I believe, their messages are essentially complementary. Even Paul, the champion of the truth that salvation comes by faith alone, tells us that God expects good works from His people (Eph. 2:10).

In his book on this theme, William Willimon says:

> *Laborare est orare* implies not that a Christian ought either to work or to pray, but that worship and work are distinct and inseparable Christian activities (*The Service of God*, Abingdon Press, p. 15).

But misunderstandings arise when people read this passage on faith and works and conclude that James is saying works are necessary or even sufficient for salvation. While James does claim that we are not saved by the kind of faith that does not show itself in good works, at *no* time does he say or imply that we are *not* saved by faith. In fact, he clearly states that salvation *is* by faith (2:23).

Dr. Frank Gaebelein sums up for me the distinction between James and Paul on this issue as well as their complementation:

> Paul deals with the root of initial acceptance with God which is wholly by grace through faith. James is concerned with the subsequent and continuing proof of the reality of the initial transaction (*Faith That Lives*, Moody Press, p. 70).

I agree. Both James and Paul believed that faith in the risen Christ brought new life, and that the inevitable result of a genuine conversion would be the works of love and justice. For both, works would never earn anyone's way to God. But once a person was established in Him, good deeds would flow out of boundless gratitude for what He had done. And both James and Paul present us with teaching that leads not to conflict, but to a bond between faith and works that should not be broken, *ever.*

Once we agree on this thesis, we can move to a practical

question. How can you and I be sure we are practicing the kind of true saving faith that is solidly joined to good works? James gives us an answer by presenting three kinds of faith, only one of which is credible.

Warren Wiersbe, in his book on James, gives a helpful outline for these verses:

James 2:14-17 deals with "Dead Faith"

James 2:18-19 deals with "Demonic Faith"

James 2:20-26 deals with "Dynamic Faith"

(From *Be Mature,* Victor Books, pp. 76-80)

Dead Faith (2:14-17)

For James, those whose faith is dead are those who talk the talk, but don't walk the walk—people who substitute words for deeds. Here he echoes the words of Jesus who said, "Not everyone who says to Me, 'Lord, Lord,' will enter into the kingdom of heaven, but only he who does the will of My Father who is *in heaven*" (Matt. 7:21).

James then illustrates his point by telling a simple story which William Barclay translates this way:

> If a brother or sister has nothing to wear and if they have not enough for their daily food, and if one of you says to them, "Go in peace," "Be warmed and fed!" and yet does not give them the essentials of bodily existence, what use is that? So, if faith too has no deeds to show, by itself it is dead.

A dear friend of mine, Jon, knows the meaning of this passage. Every day that Jon is in Washington, which as a partner in an international law firm isn't all that often, he takes the subway from his home to his office. As the door of the subway opens, the same man always stands nearby waiting and asking for money to buy food. Until recently, it was Jon's custom to give the man enough change to buy a hearty breakfast, but then Jon would go quickly on his way. One morning, however, as he pressed money into the man's hand, Jon was goaded by the conviction that he was "copping out"; the thought that "the gift without the giver is bare" came to him. He became uncomfortable—so much so that he believed God was nudging him to leave home a half hour earlier the next day in order to join the man for breakfast.

And so it has gone morning after morning. Jon and his new companion "break the fast" together. Not that Jon is always overjoyed at the prospect. Some mornings he is tired and tempted to go on to the next subway stop, avoiding his eagerly waiting friend. But Jon realizes that God has lessons for him about giving of himself as well as his substance that can only be learned through doing. Loving a neighbor as oneself requires the sometimes-inconvenient task of personal involvement. "What good are sweet words and sympathy if they have no practical effect?" The late Dr. Alfred Adler captured the essence of this idea in his maxim, "Trust only movement." By this he meant that what we really believe is judged by what we do, not by the words that roll often too glibly from our tongues.

Dr. Adler's advice brings to mind my mother's own poignant faith journey. Her mother died when she was very young, leaving her father with four small children to raise. Though my grandfather was a good man in every way and was determined to keep his family together, he realized that he had to have help. Approaching a devout woman in the church they attended, he asked if she would consider taking a job in his home to help care for the children and the house. Her forthright response was that she did not want to be "hired," but she would consider the proposal if my grandfather would take her in as his wife. I have no idea how long the negotiations lasted, but that is exactly what happened. So the four children grew up with a stepmother who, I'm certain, meant well, but who so turned my spirited mother away from the church that it was decades before she returned.

From my mother's perspective, her stepmother's religion manifested itself in an excess of rigid rules, demands, and expectations, all mixed up with a lot of sanctimonious

"God-talk." Unfortunately, very little emotional warmth or demonstration of God's love came through to my mother from her stepmother's words. Perhaps her experience was similar to John Bunyan's description of "Mr. Talkative" in *Pilgrim's Progress:*

> He talks of prayer, of repentance, of the new birth, and of faith, but he knows but only to talk of them. I have been in his family, and his house is as empty of religion as the white of an egg is of flavor.

Gratefully, this experience did not ultimately keep my mother from knowing Christ. However, it caused a long and painful detour for her, and it has served as a warning to me of the dangerous and costly discrepancy that arises when faith is verbalized but not lived out.

Demonic Faith (2:18-19)

Demons were not strangers to the world in which Jesus ministered any more than they are strangers in ours, though today we call them by other names. Jesus often cast out demons and empowered His disciples to do the same. But even though demons were familiar enough to the Jewish Christians, I would guess that James surprised them by what he said next: "You believe that there is one God. Good! Even the demons believe that—and shudder" (v. 19).

Demons have faith. They believe! They believe *in God*! They also believe in Christ (Mark 3:11-12) and they recognize Him as Judge (Mark 5:1-13). They believe and shudder. Indeed, their faith involves their understanding *and* their emotions, yet it does not yield good works. In fact, the demons' knowledge of God is deliberately turned against His good purposes, working to hinder them and anyone who has chosen to walk in trust and obedience. This is a far cry from the genuine "lived out" faith of which James spoke.

Dynamic Faith (2:20-26)

For James, dynamic faith results in a changed life and is

inseparably connected to good works. To illustrate this truth, James uses the example of two Old Testament characters who are wonderful studies in contrast. Their backgrounds and styles of life couldn't be more different, yet in the way they lived out their faith they demonstrated a profound similarity that made their faith credible.

> Was not our ancestor Abraham considered righteous for what he did when he offered his son Isaac on the altar? You see that his faith and his actions were working together, and his faith was made complete by what he did. And the Scripture was fulfilled that says, "Abraham believed God, and it was credited to him as righteousness," and he was called God's friend. You see that a person is justified by what he does and not by faith alone.
>
> In the same way, was not even Rahab the prostitute considered righteous for what she did when she gave lodging to the spies and sent them off in a different direction? As the body without the spirit is dead, so faith without deeds is dead (James 2:21-26).

Abraham, who radically and movingly demonstrated his faith when he offered his son Isaac on the altar, was "considered righteous" by that act of faith. It was by that deed that Abraham's faith was "made complete." There is no question here that James sees works as the outward sign of a deep commitment and inner faith.

In the same way, Rahab's outward action is evidence of her inner faith. However, in both examples we must remind ourselves that the starting point for good works is *always* faith. For James this is a fundamental assumption whenever he mentions genuine good works, and I am so convinced *this* is the underlying truth his critics forget. For James, any separation of works from faith in Jesus, His Risen Lord, leads to works bankrupt of spiritual meaning. Still, faith finds its *completion* in outward expressions, and that truth cannot be discarded in order to affirm the primary place of faith.

Do you, like me, find something heartwarming and hu-

man in James' choice of two such extreme examples of
faith? Abraham the wealthy, noble patriarch, and Rahab the
Gentile prostitute, "with a past." Most likely your life falls
somewhere in-between these two extremes, as mine does.
But it is reassuring to know that there is room for each one
of us on the continuum of God's chosen people, regardless
of background or present status. God's love is so totally
inclusive!

The privilege of claiming our place among those who
demonstrate inner faith with outward action is also accompanied by a great responsibility. For while we enjoy boundless hope from the assurance of salvation through faith we
run up against one of the toughest challenges of Christian
living. In the words of John Wesley, "The problem of problems is to get Christianity put into practice."

Last night I awoke sometime between midnight and dawn
with these words of Wesley's whirling around in my mind.
As I lay there, God guided my thoughts to examples of
people I know and love who are successfully linking their
faith in Christ with practice.

I thought of someone from the distant past, the mother of
four of our valued, long-time friends. Mrs. Harvey is now in
her 90s and lives in a retirement home in the West. On a
trip to California recently I visited her. I was touched by
her decision to move into a small single room with a bath,
the simplest accommodations her retirement community
offers. Crowded into that frugal space was her bed, cooking
corner, and mementos from her large and gracious home of
the past.

Later when Louie and I were talking with one of her sons,
he told us, with great affection and pride that this move had
been very important to his mother. For this was Mrs. Harvey's one way of having money left from her fixed monthly
income to support the many ministries she believes in. No
longer able to "do things," she could still pray—and give.
Her son then told us about the large gifts she is able to
contribute regularly to a hunger program and a favorite

evangelistic association, not because she is a wealthy woman but because she has made a conscious decision—a *choice,* to live sacrificially on behalf of others. And she does it with overflowing joy. Now that is putting faith into practice!

Another example of faith completed by works came to me from the life of someone we met 30 years ago and whose influence is with us still. Louie and I had gone to Scotland where he was to complete his graduate studies at New College, Edinburgh. Though we had spent two summers in work camps overseas after World War II, this time we were to be away from home and family for *two years.* Our sense of separation was also heightened by the imminent arrival of our first child.

At New College, Louie's advisor and New Testament professor was Dr. James S. Stewart, a well known and highly respected theologian and preacher. Without a doubt, Dr. Stewart was a man of great gifts and discipline and, above all, of power uniquely born of the Holy Spirit. Though the intensity of Professor Stewart's presence was unmistakable, he was a deeply humble and thoughtful man. With their countless expressions of kindness, he and his lovely wife Rosamund warded off our homesickness.

One expression of thoughtfulness touched us more than all the others. Our son Dan was about six weeks old and Louie had just started filling the pulpit in a little country church every Sunday. Naturally, we wanted to have Dan baptized there, and you might guess who we wanted to perform the service. But we just didn't have the heart to ask, especially since getting to the church was no easy task. It meant 45 minutes in a little bus over bumpy roads and around hairpin turns in usually frigid weather. Neither we nor the Stewarts had the luxury of a car in postwar Britain, and we felt it was too great an inconvenience to ask them to join us on the long bus ride. Besides, Dr. Stewart was such a busy man. So when a friend of ours at New College offered to do the service, we gratefully accepted.

When we arrived at the church I was taken to the vestry, and then at the appropriate time in the service I was led down the aisle with Dan in my arms. Out of the corner of my eye I thought I recognized someone sitting in the rear of the church. After the baptism I turned to walk back down the aisle, and this time I got a better look. My first impression was right—it was Professor Stewart. He had heard that Dan was going to be baptized and had come all that way— *just to be there.* After the service, he slipped away as quietly as he had come. And in that act, and in countless others like it, he and Ros taught us more about putting our faith into practice than all his sermons combined.

I am reminded here of the words of Edgar Guest:

> I'd rather see a sermon
> than hear one any day;
> I'd rather one should walk with me
> than merely tell the way....
> The lecture you deliver may be
> very wise and true,
> But I'd rather get my lessons
> by observing what you do.
> For I might misunderstand you
> and the high advice you give,
> But there's no misunderstanding
> how you act and how you live.

As the body without the spirit is dead, so faith without deeds is dead (James 2:26).

Once again, this is not a matter of works over faith, nor are we presented with a potential conflict. James is merely stressing the connection between two essential elements of Christianity. He is telling us that ours is a twin Gospel involving a "both-and," not an "either-or" issue.

Louie preached a sermon recently in which he spoke of the separation between faith and works as the "damnable dichotomy of our day." Similarly James shouts to us, *pleads* with us to resist such a division, and his simple message is this: For the disciples of Jesus Christ, faith and works cannot be separated—ever! And the world is waiting to see such faith—lived out in us!

> *Our Father,*
> *May we both believe and be-in-life according to*
> *Your will for us. Amen.*

Not many of you should presume to be teachers, my brothers and sisters, because you know that we who teach will be judged more strictly. We all stumble in many ways. If anyone is never at fault in what he says, he is a perfect man, able to keep his whole body in check.

When we put bits into the mouths of horses to make them obey us, we can turn the whole animal. Or take ships as an example. Although they are so large and are driven by strong winds, they are steered by a very small rudder wherever the pilot wants to go. Likewise the tongue is a small part of the body, but it makes great boasts. Consider what a great forest is set on fire by a small spark. The tongue also is a fire, a world of evil among the parts of the body. It corrupts the whole person, sets the whole course of his life on fire, and is itself set on fire by hell.

All kinds of animals, birds, reptiles and creatures of the sea are being tamed and have been tamed by man, but no man can tame the tongue. It is a restless evil, full of deadly poison.

With the tongue we praise our Lord and Father, and with it we curse men, who have been made in God's likeness. Out of the same mouth come praise and cursing. My brothers, this should not be. Can both fresh water and salt water flow from the same spring? My brothers, can a fig tree bear olives, or a grapevine bear figs? Neither can a salt spring produce fresh water.

EIGHT

THE TONGUE: TROUBLEMAKER OR TRANSFORMED BY GOD?

I find James warmly and approachably human in this passage: "We all (including me) make mistakes, and the man who does not make any mistakes in what he says is a perfect man." If I take a little liberty here, I see a twinkle in his eye as though he is *really* saying, "And you and I *both* know there is no such perfect person."

In commenting on this passage dealing with the tongue, Dr. Frank Gaebelein brought out a point which I found very interesting. The Greek word James used in this instance was the less common word for man, *aner,* which means "man *apart* from woman." Perhaps this means James did not believe women were the chief offenders in the matters of the tongue, which would be something of a switch from our unflattering stereotype.

Anthropos is the Greek word James uses overwhelmingly throughout his book to refer to mankind in general. Because of his use of this word, I have taken the liberty to add *sisters* when James speaks to the brothers, for I am convinced that James was including women in that inclusive term.

But whatever the significance of this more exclusive term *aner,* we women certainly shouldn't consider ourselves off

the hook by any means! Women are without a doubt in-
cluded in the total context of James' warning on the
tongue, even if we may not be singled out in this instance.
So men, women, those who teach by speaking or example—
all of us need to hear James clearly, for "we all stumble in
many ways."

Among the people who made up the early church, more
than a few apparently aspired to be teachers and leaders.
Here James reminds us that not everyone is called to teach,
and those who are will be judged by a higher standard, for
theirs is a most serious responsibility.

James was saying in essence, "Watch it! We are all open
to making mistakes." The word James uses means to "slip-
up," and William Barclay notes here that sin is so often not
deliberate, but the "result of a slip-up when we are off-
guard." Sadly, when leaders slip, many lives are affected. So
James reminds those in places of leadership of their special
accountability to God and to those whom they instruct.

But that isn't all, for surely James is speaking truth in a
broader sense. He is also addressing those of us who are
parents and teach by example, and indeed everyone who
claims the name of Christ. We *all* teach through our words
and actions whether consciously or not and in turn, we are
all accountable to God and to the others in our lives.

Small but Mighty

When we put bits into the mouths of horses to make
them obey us, we can turn the whole animal. Or take
ships as an example. Although they are so large and are
driven by strong winds, they are steered by a very
small rudder wherever the pilot wants to go. Likewise
the tongue is a small part of the body, but it makes
great boasts. Consider what a great forest is set on fire
by a small spark (James 3:3-5).

In these verses, James paints some vivid pictures of things
that are small but mighty. A small bit is all a rider needs to
control a powerful horse. A rudder, relatively minute, con-

trols a great ship. And so the tongue, a tiny bit of flesh in our bodies, has disproportionately mighty power, both for good and for evil in our lives.

In his study of James, Warren Wiersbe talks about the contrary forces both the bit and rudder must overcome— the wild nature of the horse and the powerful winds and currents of the sea. In the same way, he says, the tongue must overcome contrary forces, for "we have an old nature that wants to control us and make us sin. There are circumstances around us that would make us say things we ought not to say. Sin on the inside and pressures on the outside are seeking to get control of the tongue" (*Be Mature,* Victor Books, pp. 91-92).

People, it seems, have not changed fundamentally in 2,000 years. The Jewish Christians to whom James wrote must have been remarkably like us in their inability to control their tongues. James, who always spoke to the practical need, urged his readers to be "swift to hear, slow to speak" (1:19, KJV). He then accentuated his warning by adding that the person who does not bridle the tongue is not truly religious (1:26).

And James was on solid ground when he said that all through Scripture, reference is made to the dangers that reside in our words—the enslaving nature of ugly talk, profanity, idle chatter, malicious gossip, lies, etc. But nowhere is the teaching on the tongue stronger and clearer than in James 3.

The human tongue is physically small, but it yields tremendous power. And, in our hearts, we know James is not exaggerating. The joy—*and* anguish—we can cause those around us by the way we use or misuse our tongues should be something we are aware of day in and day out. Remember the little jingle we chanted so glibly as children?

Sticks and stones may break my bones,
But words can never hurt me!

We believed it . . . until one day our words betrayed us, and we knew they were not true. Perhaps it was a careless statement or a thoughtless rumor—and the hurtful spark that met dry tinder was soon raging out of control. Eventually the fire was quenched, but only after lives had been scorched and damaged—perhaps your own life, perhaps someone else's.

Charles Swindoll, in *Growing Strong in the Seasons of Life*, describes the tongue as an unguided missile:

> Restraint of the tongue is a mark of wisdom. It is a slippery eel in need of being in check between our cheeks. . . . Removing restraint from your life may seem like an exciting adventure, but it inevitably leads to tragedy. It's a lot like removing the brakes from your car. That may be daring and filled with thrills for awhile, but injury is certain. Take away the brakes and your life, like your car, is transformed into an unguided missile—destined for disaster (Multnomah Press, p. 277).

No wonder God, through His servant James, warns us of the dangers of an unconverted tongue, for both victim and abuser are wounded. Or, in James' stinging words, "The tongue is set on fire by hell itself, and can turn our whole lives into a blazing flame of destruction and disaster" (3:6, TLB).

"Consider what a great forest is set on fire by a small spark" is true not only for us personally—but globally as well. My mind turns immediately to an obvious example, that of Adolph Hitler, for surely in his life we saw personified the power of words given over to evil use. Look at the words of Larry Thomas, from a critique of George Steiner's novel based on Hitler's life:

> Steiner, a Jew, has drawn sharp criticism from many quarters for his book. And yet, his point is frighteningly clear: The power of the tongue—of language—is terrifying in its possibilities for good or evil. Just as the word can speak, and bring all things into creation, so can words destroy, twist, distort, and annihilate. *The Portage to San Cristobal of A.H.* is a frightening

tract on the restless evil of the human tongue and
spirit (Book review from *The Wittenberg Door*).

The Paradox of the Tongue

Surely, one of the most frightening aspects of this "restless
evil" is that it is so difficult to control. In fact, James flatly
states that it is impossible!

> All kinds of animals, birds, reptiles and creatures of the
> sea are being tamed and have been tamed by man, but
> no man can tame the tongue. It is a restless evil, full of
> deadly poison. With the tongue we praise our Lord and
> Father, and with it we curse men, who have been
> made in God's likeness. Out of the same mouth come
> praise and cursing. My brothers, this should not be
> (3:7-10).

Here we see the paradox of the tongue, and in the words
of William Barclay there is within us "something of the ape
and something of the angel, something of the hero and
something of the villain, something of the saint and much of
the sinner. It is James' conviction that nowhere is this con-
tradiction more evident than in the tongue."

It can blaspheme
  hurt
  intimidate
  implicate
  exaggerate
  flatter
  murmur
  and lie.
But it can also instruct
  affirm
  praise
  speak truth
  and be a powerful instrument of blessing, healing, and
  love.

And sometimes, almost in the same breath, we both bless
and curse. One of my friends with a large brood of little

ones, laughs about the way she talks about God in her Sunday School class and then yells at her children all the way home in the car. She laughs, but I know it troubles her and she is going to the right Person for help. But her situation, magnified, symbolizes too much of life for too many of us. And to this James says, "Brothers, sisters, this ought not be so."

But, if no one can tame the tongue—if, humanly speaking, we are doomed to fail on this crucial front—*where* do we get the help we need to make our words instruments of good rather than evil? How can what we say bless rather than curse our world?

While James has deftly focused our minds on the inherent problems of the tongue, we must look to Jesus for an answer to the dilemma. The truth is, I found this section on the tongue not only tough, but depressing—until I remembered that our Lord said, "What is impossible with men is possible with God" (Luke 18:27).

Our answer is not to retreat into a monastery of silence, or walk through life fearful of every word we speak. Rather, our answer lies with God, for He is eager for us to trust Him to guide our use of this potential troublemaker as we submit our lives (*including* our tongues) to Him each day. And we are in good company as we do this. Centuries ago the psalmist said, "Set a watch, O Lord, before my mouth, keep the door of my lips" (Ps. 141:3, KJV).

Our words truly reflect the content of our hearts. Shakespeare too had keen insight on this issue: "He hath a heart as sound as a bell, and his tongue is a clapper; for what the heart thinks the tongue speaks." And these echoed the words of Jesus, "Out of the abundance of the heart the mouth speaks" (Matt. 12:34, KJV).

Psalm 19:14 ties these strands of thought together. "Let the words of my mouth, and the meditation of my heart, be acceptable in Thy sight, O Lord, my strength and my redeemer" (KJV).

Our *words,* our *thoughts,* our *hearts* . . . inseparably

linked! And the *Lord* is our strength, redeeming this power-ful trio from any evil use to His good and acceptable pur-pose. And how is this possible? Only by wholly depending on God, and becoming convinced that we cannot maintain control on our own—*ever!* More and more the bottom line for me is that God means for us to trust *Him,* and not ourselves!

The insight that "the tongue can be controlled, but never cured" must be fixed in our consciousness. Daily, hourly—we need to trust every part of our lives to God. Then as His Spirit directs us, we can enjoy that special freedom, know-ing that what is impossible for us is possible with God.

Praise—Our Purpose

It is not enough to simply have tongues free of evil. They are free in order to fulfill their high purpose. And that pur-pose means communicating deep and caring feelings on the human level, and praising God and speaking for Him in sensitive loving ways.

In *Faith That Lives,* Dr. Gaebelein aptly sums up our frailty in using our tongues for their intended purpose:

"O for a thousand tongues to sing my great Redeemer's praise!"

Futile wish! We shall never have a thousand tongues. If we had them we should not know what to do with them—not when the one we have is so strongly silent respecting the Lord who loves us and gave Himself for us.

Isn't that true! We are pathetically slow in speaking up for the Lord with those around us—and so sadly reticent to give voice to the praise He *deserves,* and *desires.*

The psalmist urges us to bless "the name of the Lord from this time forth and for evermore. From the rising of the sun unto the going down of the same the Lord's name is to be praised" (Ps. 113:2-3, KJV).

The Lord inhabits the praise of His people. How unaware we seem to be that praise *pleases* Him!

And though we should praise Him for Himself alone—
there is no question that praise is for our benefit as well.
For praise releases all sorts of healthy forces in our lives.

Years ago in Louie's more perfectionistic days when he
was a frantically busy young pastor, he suffered from migraine headaches that simply knocked him out. Nothing any
doctor prescribed reached the pain and we were becoming
more and more discouraged. Then, one Sunday night, during an unusually busy period, Louie was preparing for the
evening meeting in our home when the dreaded happened—a migraine hit. Stretched out on the bed in a dark-
ened room, he could hear the sounds of happy conversation
coming from the people already gathered in our living
room and, totally miserable, he began to pray, "Lord, help!"
Then in words he could understand, if not hear, a dialogue
began:

> "You're tired, aren't you, Louie?"
> "Oh *yes,* Lord—so tired."
> "Then either you are trying to do more than I mean
> for you to do, or you are not taking My strength for the
> task I have called you to do."

Silence—pain—and more silence. Finally, a sharp and unmistakable command,

> "Louie, *praise* Me!"
> "I don't feel like it, Lord."
> And again, "Praise Me!"

The moments, he recalls, seemed like hours as Louie
wrestled with his will. Finally mustering every ounce of
energy he could at that moment, he made a choice, an
"attitudinal decision," he called it, to be obedient to God in
spite of how he felt. Amid the nausea, the pain, and the
throbbing brain, he made himself get up from the bed, and
almost staggering, he went to the bathroom to wash his face
and comb his hair. While he stood there, Louie began singing a simple chorus of praise. Never feeling less like singing
in his life—he did it anyway. The misery persisted. He made
his way down the dark hall and, in obedience, opened the

door to our crowded, light-filled living room. As the evening service began, an expression of near oblivion washed Louie's face. He chose three hymns of praise, and as he led us, sang each word with sincerity and deliberation.

As he recounted later, it was not a matter of feeling—it was a spiritual discipline; an exercise in obedience that exacted from him every bit of his remaining energy. And what happened next was, for Louie, a miracle. The last hymn of praise was sung, and his headache was gone—totally. What is more, that was the last migraine Louie ever had. Over the years there have been times when he has felt "on the verge," but he has made that same "attitudinal decision" to praise God. Again and again, praise has released God's healing power in his life. At the same time, Louie has been compelled to take an honest look at the pace he is keeping, for learning to praise God freely has meant submitting an overly busy schedule and sometimes unrealistic set of goals to the Lord.

Together, we have learned that praise is the key to rejuvenation when the "slough of despond" strikes either of us. I love the passage in Isaiah that says, "The Spirit of the Lord God is upon me . . . to appoint unto them that mourn . . . the garment of *praise* for the spirit of heaviness" (Isa. 61:1, 3, KJV).

Praise releases healing and joy. Praise is life-giving! I'm convinced!

How clearly we see that our tongues need to be transformed in order to fulfill their highest purpose, but God makes this possible only through the transformation of our very *lives,* through Jesus Christ. In this way, ours is not a problem rooted in the tongue but in the heart, for, "Those things which proceed out of the mouth come forth from the heart" (Matt. 15:18, KJV) and "out of [the heart] are the issues of life" (Prov. 4:23, KJV).

We can stubbornly possess our own hearts and battle daily with our tongue, or we can *surrender* our hearts to Christ and let Him control every part of us—body, mind, and spirit as we abide in Him. The choice is ours.

The following prayer written by Louie's father and my first and much-loved pastor may encourage you, as it has me, to—day by day—accept the miracle of heart transformation.

O Christ,

A walk with Thee will make a difference. Our speech will betray us then; we shall come upon the dialect of heaven, and our accents of love will disclose the fact that we belong to another Country. A new life will give us a new vocabulary; our verbs will take on a new vitality of love, and a new spirit will captain our speech.

We shall acquire the habit of praise, and in every hour shall something good be said. All vehemence of speech shall then stem from our hatred of wrong, never of the evil-doer, and our words shall fall like a gentle rain from heaven upon a field of humanity parched for praise and for love.

In this holy trait, make us like our Lord today, more like the Master. With our heads raised to Thee in holy supplication, we plead for this miracle that will touch our tongues and change our speech. Work this miracle of the new life in us, O Christ. May the world see that our religion works, and having heard what falls from our lips, cry out, "Thou hast been with the Galilean—thy speech betrayeth thee!" Amen.

Brothers and sisters, do not slander one another. Anyone who speaks against his brother or judges him speaks against the law and judges it. When you judge the law, you are not keeping it, but sitting in judgment on it. There is only one Lawgiver and Judge, the One who is able to save and destroy. But you—who are you to judge your neighbor?

NINE
SLANDER & JUDGMENT

To a child of 4, it was a confusing and difficult time. My parents had gone through a painful separation, and my father had simply disappeared from our lives. Out of necessity, my mother took a job, and we moved to a new neighborhood to be near a woman who had offered to watch me while my mother worked.

One day, soon after we arrived, a gang of neighborhood children gathered in front of the tiny duplex where we lived and called me out to play. Eagerly, I joined them on the lawn.

Apparently, word had spread through the block that the new people who had moved into their territory were a bit "different"—for in *that* time and *that* place, a young mother and daughter living alone were an unusual combination.

At any rate, I was placed in the middle of the yard and the other children joined hands and made a circle around me. Then they began to skip and chant:

Colleen doesn't have a daddy,
Colleen doesn't have a daddy.

We didn't live in that neighborhood very long, but years after we moved I was still wrestling with the impact of those words. That casual experience made me aware at a young age of the sting careless words can cause. I deter-mined to be careful to *think* about what I said to people—and what I said to others *about* them.

When I was a bit older I even wrote poems that spoke of my disdain for gossip and careless talk. When I read my childhood diary and come across those verses today, I un-derstandably find them naive and childish. But at the same time I am touched that the underlying truth I was express-ing at seven years of age still holds for me in my fifties. I am just as convinced today that words, carelessly spoken, can harm and destroy.

In the last chapter we saw how strongly James felt about the dangers of an unconverted tongue. In this chapter we wil look at one of the specific ways we misuse our tongues when we indulge in gossip, thereby judging our sisters and brothers in life.

Choice Morsels

Paul speaks about gossip as a sin seen among unbelievers that he *feared* he would find in the community of believers (Rom. 1:29; 2 Cor. 12:20). There are, in fact, few sins that the Bible hits harder than evil, irresponsible talk. People of every age can witness to the heartbreaking, devastating fall-out from carelessly spoken words.

Jesus rebuked the Pharisees, saying, "But I tell you that men will have to give account on the day of judgment for every careless word they have spoken. For by your words you will be acquitted, and by your words you will be con-demned" (Matt. 12:36-37). Those are harsh words our Lord spoke and the psalmist isn't any easier on us: "Whoever slanders his neighbor in secret, him will I put to silence" (Ps. 101:5). And in his wisdom, Solomon tells us that gossip is not a superficial activity: "The words of a gossip are like choice morsels; they go down to a man's inmost parts" (Prov. 26:22).

I suspect I have always been something of a crusader against gossip. When I was in junior high, spending hours of every day talking with friends on the phone, I taped a little reminder on the wall:

The friend who gossips *with* you will gossip *of* you.

In high school I remember telling off the "big man on campus" one day when he continued to speak derogatorily—and publicly—about anyone who didn't fit into his mold of what was "cool."

So it was interesting—and even a little symbolic to me— that when I began working as a teenager under contract to Twentieth Century Fox, my first substantial role was in a film that dealt with the subject of gossip. The story was based on a best-selling novel by Paul Wellman called *The Walls of Jericho.* It took place at the turn of the century, in a small mid-Western town called Jericho—and the "walls" were built of evil gossip that imprisoned people in a miserable existence within that narrow community.

I played the role of Margie, a teenaged girl whose life was plagued by gossip that followed her everywhere because she had been born out of wedlock—and the whole town knew it. When she was sixteen, the talk became so painful for her she decided to run away from home, and leave Jericho behind forever. Disguised as a boy, she made her way to the train station late one night. There, waiting to hop a freight, she was recognized by the town drunk who pursued, and finally cornered her in a remote, dark storage area behind the station. Grabbing the nearest thing at hand to defend herself, Margie swung a shovel wildly in the man's direction. Intending only to stop him, she struck a fatal blow to his head—and he fell dead at her feet.

The rest of the story centered around Margie's trial—and defense—and there is no need to bore you with all the melodramatic details. (Every scene, but one, called for me to shed tears—buckets of them!)

Suffice it to say that with the help of two lawyers who defended and befriended her, Margie found that her answer was not in running away from the pain of gossip—but in facing it head-on. The way out was the way through!

Strange, just thinking again about that old movie makes me realize I enjoyed working on it more than any of the others that followed in my short four year career. For though it was by no means a "religious" movie, its message was, for me, spiritual—and one in which I deeply believed. For gossip and careless words *can* cut deep into a person's life, and God means for His people to be both kind *and* responsible in the way they talk.

Charles Simeon, a 19th century minister in Cambridge, wrote a friend some good advice on how to cope with gossip. Though the date on the letter was 1817, Simeon's advice is just as relevant for us today as it was then. The three points I want most to remember from what he wrote are:

> Never to drink into the spirit of one who circulates an ill report.
>
> Always to moderate, as far as I can, the unkindness which is expressed toward others.
>
> Always to believe, that if the other side were heard, a very different account would be given of the matter (Derek Prime, *From Trials to Triumph,* Regal Books, p. 115).

If only we could grasp the effect and extent of our careless words. But it is impossible to know how many hearts have been broken, marriages damaged, friendships ruptured, and reputations ruined by cruel, irresponsible talk. But, as much as it hurts, we *need not* be devastated. God is always ready to help us work through the painful results of loose and thoughtless tongues—and He is there to touch those destructive experiences with insight and healing.

Sara's Story

My friend's face spoke volumes. Dark circles under her swollen eyes witnessed convincingly of sleepless nights, and her pained expression told me she was going through some dreadful valley.

As we sat in the quiet of her living room, her story began

to unfold. Several years earlier, my friend, whom I will call Sara, had become part of a small, tightly knit Christian community. In the beginning, she was very enthusiastic about her new spiritual family and spent virtually all of her non-working and non-sleeping hours involved in one way or another at her church. Her life, which had been rather quiet and unembellished, was now consumed by her new commitment. So much so that she lost touch with her old friends and focused completely on the new people in her life.

According to the rule of the community, she was assigned to a small circle of people who had an "elder" who ruled over them—not only in spiritual matters, but in every facet of their lives. (At that point in our conversation I began to get very uncomfortable!)

As Sara described the inner working of that group and the complicated web it had spun around her life, I was appalled! While I am in *full* agreement with loving, caring support groups within the body of Christ, *this* was a totally different thing. Instead of being "enabled," she was being manipulated—and it seemed to me, she had completely lost her own sense of God's guidance in her life. Choosing God's way for herself was not an option, for she was *told* what "God's" way was and she was not to question her group or especially her "elder's" judgment.

She was a prisoner in that tenacious web, and her group members were using evil methods of gossip, slander, and judgment to keep her there. Feigning authority, they were invading the prerogatives only God should have had in Sara's life—and she was being deeply hurt—even torn apart by their misguided domination.

As we talked, Sara decided to resist her urge to retreat from the community in favor of going back to "speak the truth in love." It may work and it may not, and Sara knows that. Either way, she is going to need lots of prayer, love, friendship, and healing. For slander and judgment have cut deep into her life and, at this point, there is no tidy, happy ending—for Sara's story is still happening.

This type of judgment is the focus of James 4:11. The Greek word James uses, *katalalain,* means "harsh, unloving, censorious," literally "invading the prerogatives of others." It is an evil form of judging where we assume a kind of superior attitude and authority, a pretense to know and judge when we are not qualified to do either. James makes it crystal clear that this kind of attitude and behavior is WRONG!

What James says on this subject is hard-hitting and in direct contrast to the common notion many have today that gossip and judging are among the "lesser" sins—not very serious when lined up against the major "don'ts". We'd have a difficult time convincing my friend Sara that a "lesser" sin could cause her such deep pain. And even more important, the Scriptures soundly contradict that notion.

When we slander and judge a brother or sister, it is the same as being in contempt of Christ's law of love by presuming, as it were, to judge it. And how true that is, for when we speak evil things about others, we *are* judging them, which must be why slander and judging are so often linked in Scripture. When we treat brothers and sisters this way, we are indeed denying Christ's command to love others as we love ourselves and we are, in fact, playing right into the devil's hand.

> There is only one Lawgiver and Judge, the One who is
> able to save and destroy (James 4:12).

As I work on this passage, we have just celebrated Holy Week. There has been a remarkably fine series on televison based on the life of Jesus. Perhaps you saw it too and remember the scene. The Crucifixion is approaching. Pilate is with Jesus and he asks, "Do You not know that I have the power to crucify You, and the power to release You?" And Jesus replies, "You have no power at all against Me, except it were given you from above." (See John 19:10-11.)

The scene, taken from Scripture, was a potent reminder that the final power to judge, in *all* things, belongs to God;

when we gossip, slander, and judge, we are disobedient usurpers. Disobedient to the royal law of Jesus and usurpers of a role reserved for God. My father-in-law, Dr. Louis Evans, Sr., put it well when he wrote, "This is the tragic conceit that leads a man to sit himself down on the bench beside God, that persuades him to put on the judicial robe and predicate to himself the wisdom to judge the rest of humanity" (*Make Your Faith Work*, Revell, p. 98). Actually, God allows no one to get away with assuming His prerogatives, and His judgment is on us when we try.

How Dare You Judge!

James ends this passage with a question: "But you—who are you to judge your neighbor?" (4:12) Once again, James speaks in a way reminiscent of his brother. Remember the question Jesus asked, "How can you say to your brother or sister, 'Let me take the speck out of your eye,' when all the time there is a plank in your own eye?" (Matt. 7:4)

What a graphic way of telling us to look to the sin in our own lives when we are about to judge someone else. If we could only learn to do this *one* thing, I believe it would deliver us from the dangerous tendency within each of us to censure others.

Last night I was watching the television news when, as part of the Washington reelection year coverage, there was an "exposé" of the way one of our government officials has been handling his personal finances. The news report zeroed in on one specific embarrassment to the politician. While it was clear that what he had done was not in violation of the law, he was, nonetheless, made to look highly irresponsible and the viewer was left with lots of questions. Defending himself on camera, the official claimed no wrongdoing, describing his mistakes as an oversight—that was all. And the culprit he claimed to be responsible? His extremely busy schedule.

In my heart I had supported him up to that point, but when he blamed his schedule for his oversight, a judging spirit welled up within me and I heard myself say sarcastically, *"Oh, come on now! You've got to be kidding!"*

But the words were no sooner out of my mouth when I got a spiritual "poke in the ribs" that reminded me of a situation years before in my own life.

Louie and I had gone through an agonizing period of ministry in the church we then served—literally moving from one crisis to another, including murder, suicide, drug-overdose, and several tragic teenage deaths. As I look back now, I know it was God's grace—His grace *alone*—that provided the emotional energy to see us through that trying season of stress—and the amazing opportunities for ministry it provided. During those months we repeatedly scheduled time ahead in our calendar to take care of family business, finances, and the like, and yet another emergency would hit someone in our church, and off we would go to be with another family in trauma. The emotional involvement we felt with our people was very real and it took its toll. We became weary . . . and finally exhausted.

When events quieted down, we had symptoms of battle fatigue and our personal business affairs were in shambles. Bills overdue, extra interest to pay, difficult letters of explanation to write, calls to make. We scrambled to make things right and told ourselves, *No conscious wrongdoing . . . an oversight, a mistake . . . that's all.* And the culprit we blamed? Our extremely busy schedule, of course!

As I sat in front of the television and remembered that draining season of our lives, a wave of emotion came over me. The same chagrin and embarrassment Louie and I had felt then when we realized how we had allowed the state of *our* business affairs to deteriorate was with me again. In that humbled state, the words of Jesus came to me, "How can you say to your brother, take the speck out of your eye, when there is a log in your own?"

I no longer had the urge to be sarcastic about that man on the screen in front of me. In fact, I felt ashamed. And isn't it true? The very qualities that we most quickly criticize in others are often the qualities that can be found in us.

And this does not mean that we are not to acknowledge right and wrong and deal with it. We *must,* whether in ourselves or in others. Rather, it has to do with our *attitude* about our neighbor who falls and reminds us that the possibility and tendency to fall is within us all.

Spiritual Sensitivity

Louie and I have a friend who has made a commitment to Christ in recent years. His background before becoming a Christian was rough, tough, and almost totally secular. He didn't have much help growing up and he got into a lot of bad habits. Now that he is a Christian, he's different, but he is "in process" and like all of us, he is not yet perfect. He still has lots of rough edges—and raises a lot of religious eyebrows.

But those who take time to really look at him realize how much our friend has grown in the Lord in a relatively short time. They do not judge him—they love him. And in loving him they are fulfilling Christ's royal law in their own lives and encouraging a brother to grow in his journey with Christ.

We tend to judge people because we often fail to see where they have come from. We judge them at a given moment and may never see how far they have come or the direction they are heading. Kahlil Gibran pushes us to look beyond the surface: "Let him who would lash the offender look unto the spirit of the offended. . . . The guilty is often the victim of the injured. . . . And if any of you would punish in the name of righteousness and lay the ax unto the evil tree, let him see to its roots" (*The Prophet,* Alfred Knopf Publishers, pp. 44-45).

We are all members of one body and each member belongs to all the others. In all our personal relationships, we need to "speak the truth in love" with the goal of edifying the body. Paul calls us to be change agents for godliness in one another's lives, without falling into the temptation of judging. This is where we need discernment—a real sensitivity in the spirit—so we can be as "wise as serpents and as innocent as doves" in all our relationships (Matt. 10:16, RSV).

May God help us all to so love—and to encourage others along the way.

> *Our Father,*
> *Your love has warned us to "judge not"—so that*
> *we ourselves will not be judged. Keep us in*
> *touch with our deep and constant need for Your*
> *mercy, and help us extend that same spirit of*
> *mercy and generosity to others. Keep us mindful*
> *that "mercy cannot get in, where mercy goes not*
> *out." Amen.*

What causes fights and quarrels among you? Don't they come from your desires that battle within you? You want something but don't get it. You kill and covet, but you cannot have what you want. You quarrel and fight.

If you harbor bitter envy and selfish ambition in your hearts, do not boast about it or deny the truth. Such "wisdom" does not come down from heaven but is earthly, unspiritual, of the devil. For where you have envy and selfish ambition, there you find disorder and every evil practice. But the wisdom that comes from heaven is first of all pure; then peace loving, considerate, submissive, full of mercy and good fruit, impartial and sincere. Peacemakers who sow in peace raise a harvest of righteousness.

You do not have, because you do not ask God.

TEN

GOD'S PEACE— FOR THE HEART AND FOR THE WORLD

There is no subject James is reluctant to tackle. Here he asks one of the most difficult questions in all human history:

> What causes wars, and what causes fightings among
> you? (4:1, RSV)

And when we look at his letter, overall, we see that James is speaking about war and dissension in every area of life. James 2:1-9 talks about class war, rich versus poor, and chapter 5:1-6 deals with employers and employees. Chapter 4:11-12 talks about the strife that results from judging and gossiping, while 4:1 talks about the war within the self. ("Don't wars come from your desires that battle within?") Finally, chapter 4:4-10 gets to the core of all war—rebellion against God Himself.

There can be *no* doubt—James was concerned about war and strife on every level, and his words are every bit as relevant for us as they were for the first century Christians to whom he wrote. James gives us a strong reminder of a fact we too often forget: God, the God of our Lord Jesus Christ, is the God of peace. And as His disciples, we are to be peacemakers, which according to the Sermon on the Mount, is one of the basic characteristics of the Christian life (Matt. 5:9).

War and Its Causes

With all of our 20th century knowledge and "progress,"
theologians and philosophers speak volumes about war, its
causes, and its devastating results. Yet in a few terse statements James, who knew nothing about modern psychology,
put his finger on the root causes of war and strife. When we
find strife and wars among us, we are *not* to blame God.
God never wills it that way. If we look honestly—and deeply—we will see that it is *our* human wickedness that causes
every violent act, every outbreak of war, every disturbing
dissension among us.

I can almost hear someone challenge that thought saying,
"But in Old Testament times, didn't God sometimes allow
wars and strife to judge a nation?" Indeed, He did—and it
happens still today. But "allowing" and "willing" are very
different things. I think God *wills* peace for His people, but
in the words of Leslie Weatherhead: "What is *not* God's will
can nevertheless be His instrument."

From *A Collection of Peace Sermons* I found these words
of Vernon Grounds:

> Though James is not a sociologist, he gives us a pro-
> found analysis of why history is a terrible record of
> marching armies and bloody battles: "What causes
> wars, and what causes fightings among you? Is it not
> your passions that are at war in your members? You
> desire and you do not have; so you kill. And you covet
> and cannot obtain; so you fight and wage war" (James
> 4:1-2, RSV). Ruthless ambition, greed for land and gold
> and power, fierce hatred and cruel envy—these are the
> root causes of war. War is not caused by the will of
> God but by the wickedness of men and women who
> have strayed from God's values (From *Preaching on
> Peace,* The Other Side Book Service).

James answers his own arresting question by asking
another:

> Don't [wars] come from your desires that battle within
> you?

This implies that war begins in our emotions—that part of us that feels and reacts, that underlies the intellectual—rather than in our minds. "Wars do not start by logical combustion, they incubate in the heart." And what are these "emotions of the heart" that can do us in?

"Evil" desire and covetousness. I added the "evil," for desire can be right and a part of God's goodness in our lives. If we are abiding in Christ, we can trust that our desires are more and more His desires. Desire, in and of itself, is not wrong. But there is *evil* desire which is often seen in an inordinate and unreasonable lust to acquire.

I think it was *this* evil desire James had in mind when he said, "You desire and do not have; so you kill. And you covet and cannot obtain; so you fight and wage war' (4:2, RSV). And isn't it true? Behind most struggles is a passion to possess. It may be money, property, position, power, or a person . . . some *thing* or some *one* that is not rightfully ours.

The Bible reminds us that this has always been so. Today I was reading the Old Testament story of Eli, the priest at Shiloh, and there it was. Eli's two sons, Hophni and Phineas, coveted the sacrifices slaughtered for the altar and the women who served at the tabernacle. So they stole from the people and from God.

Nations behave like people. Countries too want to possess and manipulate other people and their lands. One of the evil desires of Nazism was wrapped up in their concept of *lebensraun*—"more space to live"—which drove them to take what did not belong to them. And even when a nation does not move out aggressively as the Third Reich did, it can still stir up trouble if it must have "the edge" in the balance of power, and maintain its position no matter how that oppresses others. In this kind of covetousness lie the seeds of war and strife. We cannot expect a lasting peace when people are exploited, for there is no peace without justice.

Bitter jealousy. One of the experiences I find most rewarding is working with other people to get a job done—I love it. Whether it is some practical ministry in the inner city, or brainstorming some creative idea for the church, or working as a family to build a place of retreat in the High Sierra. It is a great feeling to be part of a team where people are supporting one another and are not concerned about who gets the credit—because the goal is the important thing. *But,* all that happy situation needs is one jealous team member, and the goal and the credit become so fused that strife and confusion take over. Jealousy and rivalry can so quickly displace teamwork and harmony. And when that happens within the body of Christ, it is not only our task that suffers, but our witness of love as well.

Selfish ambition. Once again, I'm glad ambition is qualified, for ambition in itself is not wrong. Being sensitively aggressive and assuming servant leadership can be wonderful when it is practiced with the right motive and spirit. But *selfish* ambition is a different matter. It puts people down in order to build itself up; it criticizes, undermines, plots evil. According to the *Expositor's Bible,* the Greek word for selfish ambition, *eritheian,* means a self-seeking attitude bent on gaining advantage for oneself or one's group. It is a "selfish zeal" that poisons personal relationships and keeps the nations of the world from working together for peace.

James could not have been more on target with his warning against covetousness, jealousy, and selfish ambition. They are a deadly trio and when we allow them in our lives we are choosing "earthly wisdom . . . of the devil" as opposed to "the wisdom that comes from above." But we do not *have* to live by the world's wisdom. We have a choice.

> Every time you make a choice you are turning the central part of you, the part of you that chooses, into something a little different from what it was before. And taking your life as a whole, with all your innumerable choices, all your life long you are slowly turning this central thing either into a heaven creature or into a hellish creature; either into a creature that is

in harmony with God, and with other creatures, and with itself or else into one that is in a state of war and hatred with God, and with its fellow creatures, and with itself. To be the one kind of creature is heaven; that is, it is joy, and peace, and knowledge and power. To be the other means madness, horror, idiocy, rage, impotence, and eternal loneliness. Each of us at each moment is progressing to the one state or the other (C.S. Lewis, *Mere Christianity*).

Covetousness, jealousy, and selfish ambition can be displaced only when we *choose* to make Christ the center of our lives—when our love for Him and His cause is greater than any personal desire or ambition. When we make that choice, we reject the world's wisdom and embrace God's wisdom for our lives.

Choose God's Wisdom

How does God's wisdom from above differ from what the world purveys? Solomon said God's "wisdom is more precious than rubies" (Prov. 8:11). It is valuable because it is so practical and workable in everyday situations. It enables us to take facts and *learn* from them, in contrast to having great knowledge without being very wise about life. Many people who have not had the opportunity of education can, nevertheless, be very rich in God's wisdom.

"Ma Smith" is just such a person. I first met her several years ago when I joined a team from National Presbyterian Church who served breakfast to the growing number of hungry street people at our sister church in the inner city. Ma Smith lived a few doors from the church and would occasionally drop in to the worship and praise service that preceded the meal. After her first few visits I noticed that when Ma Smith was there, the sharing time was unusually rich. Though this 80 plus year old woman had not gone beyond the third grade, she always had something deeply profound and moving to say. And in the years since as the ministry has grown, she has become a real part of much that goes on in that block. She continues to astonish us with her colorful, practical insights into life and human nature. She has earned the reputation of wise counselor to young and old, rich and poor, black and white. Ma Smith knows God, and has been richly endowed with His wisdom.

God's wisdom is, first of all, practical, and tuned in to life. It is also "pure, then peaceable, gentle, open to reason, full of mercy and good fruits, without uncertainty or insincerity. And the harvest of righteousness is sown in peace by those who make peace" (3:17-18, RSV). Here James gives us some powerful spiritual weapons for making peace.

1. *First pure.* Purity is transparent. It is what it seems to be, all the way through. It is the absence of any wrong motivation, the opposite of self-seeking. If we are pure (honest in our motivation), jealousy and selfish ambition will not take root in our lives. We will no longer try to justify them by saying, "But that's the way the world operates." We will see them as the evils they are. To be pure means we stop fooling ourselves and trying to fool others. We will try to make our "yes" mean yes, and our "no" mean no (Matt. 5:37; James 5:12).

Soren Kierkegaard said, "To be pure in heart is to will one thing"; so purity also has to do with simplicity—a particular challenge for women! We are pulled in so many directions . . . so stretched out and exposed, like a reed responding to each breeze that blows. If we are married and have a family, we feel the needs of our husbands and children. We feel the pull of friends, church, community— and indeed, the world! Many of us also have our own work and all of us have needs that are our very own.

How difficult for us, then, to achieve a sense of simplicity in the midst of these many valid tugs at our lives, yet how necessary for spiritual growth and the healthy functioning of our lives. As we wrestle with this challenge, God's practical wisdom urges us away from multiplicity which leads to fragmentation, and toward simplicity which leads to wholeness. Our answer will not be found in withdrawing from life, but in seeking the balance between doing and being, retreat and return. If we "will one thing," we will allow God to prune away those other things which may be *good*, but are peripheral to the overall good He has for our lives.

We may make mistakes, but the direction of our lives will be right. For pure people are not perfect, but they *are* genuine, congruent, sincere, and "simple" in the best sense of the word.

2. *Peaceable.* Worldly wisdom fosters bitterness and confusion, but God's wisdom paves the way for peace. Not "peace at any price," but *real* peace that comes from the purity that wants the best for all people. When we are not driven by selfish ambition, we aren't straining and striving to do other people in. Instead there is energy to be involved in working for real peace.

And peacemakers will sometimes have to stir the water in order to bring about a true resolution in a troubling situation. The Hebrew word for peace, *shalom*, means "the peace that comes after the honest struggle."

God's wisdom makes peace possible in all our relationships. But there is no guarantee. We need to remember that when Jesus said, "Blessed are the peacemakers, for they shall be called the children of God," He followed that beatitude immediately with this promise and warning: "Blessed are they which are persecuted for righteousness' sake" (Matt. 5:9-10, KJV). I don't think this connection was accidental. When we get involved in things that make for peace, we may very well have to pay the cost. But when it comes to being God's peacemakers in the world, I don't see that we have an option. The question is not *Will we take the risk?*, but *Will we be obedient to Jesus the Lord of life?*

3. *Gentle.* Aristotle said gentleness looks "to the spirit, and not to the letter, to the intention and not to the action, to the whole and not to the part . . . it remembers the good and not the evil."

4. *Open to reason.* I love that! God's wisdom makes us approachable; the kind of people who put others at ease. "It

allows discussion and is willing to yield to others" (v. 17, TLB). Interesting that God's wisdom keeps us from the need to be the "wise one" in every situation. Our attitude will not intimidate people. How lovely! We can be open and loving with those who differ, and able to put ourselves in the other person's place. Isn't this an example of the deep practicality of God's wisdom? For when we *always have to* be right, we may very likely "win the battle" only to "lose the war."

5. *Full of mercy and good fruits.* In other words, mercy is not just one big burst of love and generosity. Mercy is the growing, *continuing* characteristic of the Christian overflowing with good works. Heavenly wisdom tells us it is part of our new nature to respond to those in need—not for thanks or to exact from the needy some desired response— but simply out of gratitude and love for what God has done. *And* in obedience to Him—until kindness and giving are part of our very essence and flow from our lives as naturally and regularly as fruit on a healthy tree.

6. *Without uncertainty or without partiality.* God's wisdom doesn't show favoritism and would never discriminate against anyone. This is one of my deep convictions that the love of Jesus Christ cures us of that kind of pre-judging of others. This allows the richness of diversity in our lives— for God's wisdom carries with it no breath of favoritism, nothing to separate us from *any* of God's other children. God's wisdom is "without insincerity," or as J.B. Phillips translated it, "with no hint of hypocrisy."

We can be so quick to criticize in others what we secretly harbor in our own lives, and that reveals a lack of sincerity in our hearts. In the international scene I believe "God's wisdom" would make us reasonable, willing to listen to each other even when we have basic disagreements, and sincere, willing to *act* reasonably and not just talk about it.

I recently received a news service bulletin in which Billy Graham, speaking about ways of working for world peace, said, "To avoid the possibility of confrontation with other super powers, I would like to see the leaders of both sides lower the rhetoric and, if possible, have summit meetings on a regular basis so they can know each other personally. That would indicate sincerity" (EP News Service, 1/7/84). I agree.

7. *The harvest of righteousness is sown in peace by those who make peace* (v. 18, RSV). I particularly like the way J.B. Phillips translates this verse. "The wise are peace-makers who go on quietly sowing for a harvest of righteous-ness—in other people, and in themselves." I envision a beautiful working-farm where peacemakers plant seeds of honest speech, love, forgiveness, reconciliation, and the fruit that results is righteousness. Peace and righteousness, then, are inseparable. We need to remind ourselves again and again that there is *no* peace without justice and righteousness. If only we could learn this and act on it, in all our personal relationships, and in our relationships among nations! God wants us to be peacemakers in our marriages, our families, our communities, our churches, our places of work, our nation, and our world!

Of course, we can never be God's peacemakers until *we* have ourselves been reconciled to God by faith in the life and death of Jesus Christ. It is by accepting what He has done for us on the cross—something we could *never* do for ourselves—that we experience the power of new life. It is only then, as people who have entered into God's peace, that we can be His agents of peace and righteousness. And as we go in that outward direction, the words of Paul to the Corinthians remind us "though we live in the world, we do not wage war as the world does. The weapons we fight with are not the weapons of the world" (2 Cor. 10:3-4). And James, ever practical, has in this passage clearly given us our own spiritual weapons for making peace.

The Weapon of Prayer

You do not have, because you do not ask (James 4:2, RSV).

Here James affirms his belief in prayer. If we are going to be peacemakers, full of God's wisdom and using His spiritual weapons for making peace, we must be people of prayer.

Prayer can never be incidental to Christian peacemaking. And those of us involved in peace issues need to learn that. Ron Sider says, "It is a tragic fact that contemporary Christian social activists often place less emphasis on prayer than contemporary Gospel evangelists" (from the Evangelicals for Social Action pamphlet, *Praying for Peace and Justice*). Richard Lovelace is right: "Most of those who are praying are not praying about social issues, and most of those who are active in social issues are not praying very much" (*Dynamics of Spiritual Life*, p. 392).

I can almost hear James shouting again at us down through the centuries: "Brothers, sisters, this ought not to be so! You do not have because you do not ask."

How much we are like the believers to whom James was writing. Busy with all kinds of things—even very good things for God—yet neglecting to be obedient to Him in prayer. I just don't think many of us are convinced that prayer is a weapon more powerful than all the weapons of war in the world.

We need to hear again God's word to us from Paul:

> I urge then . . . that requests, prayers, intercession and thanksgiving be made for everyone—for kings and all those in authority, that we may live peaceful and quiet lives in all godliness and holiness. This is good, and pleases God our Saviour, who wants all people to be saved and to come to a knowledge of the truth (1 Tim. 2:1-4).

Vernon Grounds, speaking about this passage from 1 Timothy, said:

> This is surely one of the great New Testament pronouncements on the purpose and effectiveness of prayer. We are urged to pray in order that, cooperating with God, we may establish a society of peace and quietness, a society within which the Gospel can be

freely proclaimed and people come to know Jesus Christ as Saviour. What could be plainer? (From a sermon appearing in *Preaching on Peace,* Other Side Books)

It is plain, isn't it? God wants us to be His agents of peace in the world. Our weapons are prayer and God's wisdom which is pure, peaceable, gentle, reasonable, merciful, and full of good fruit. He wants us to be "peacemakers who go on quietly sowing for a harvest of righteousness—in other people, and in ourselves."

Jesus said, "Whatever you ask for in prayer, believe that you will receive it, and it will be yours" (Matt. 11:23-24).

O Lord,
This study has fused in my mind and heart the relationship between peace and prayer. I have been convicted of not praying enough. I pray for myself, my family, my church, and the needs of those I know and love. But God, forgive me, I do not pray enough for peace, and the world You so loved that You gave everything for. Help me. I believe—help me believe more—and pray more. Amen.

My dear brothers and sisters, take note of this: Everyone should be quick to listen, slow to speak and slow to become angry, for man's anger does not bring about the righteous life that God desires. Therefore, get rid of all moral filth and the evil that is so prevalent, and humbly accept the Word planted in you, which can save you. Who is wise and understanding among you? Let him show it by his good life, by deeds done in the humility that comes from wisdom. Submit yourselves, then, to God. Resist the devil, and he will flee from you. Come near to God and He will come near to you. Wash your hands, you sinners, and purify your hearts, you double-minded. Humble yourselves before the Lord, and He will lift you up.

ELEVEN
HUMILITY

Some of the happiest people I know are those who have tried living life in their own strength—and failed. Realizing their spiritual bankruptcy, they were ready to let Someone Else take over their lives. They entered the kingdom through the door of their own need, and were met there by God's amazing grace.

My journey to that place of knowing my need was long and arduous. I grew up with a very casual attitude toward established religion. I wandered in and out of church. During my college years I hungered for more of God in my life—a God I had always believed in, but never done much about. So I looked to the church to show me the way. I joined, I worked, I tithed, I tried, and I found only frustration and weariness. "Churchianity" was not for me.

By that time I had gone from college to Hollywood, where I was put under contract to a motion picture studio and encouraged to expect a creative career. I liked the work, and for the first time in my life I had many of the things I'd always thought I wanted. Yet underneath the surface, deep down inside, the new position and the possessions that came with it added up to zero. I had "more" of everything, but "everything" was not enough. The gnawing hunger was still there. It was a time of truth for me. I had run out of ways of trying to work my way to God. For the first time I was in touch with my deep inner need, and was ready to admit it—and to reach out.

God's timing is so perfect. At that most vulnerable season in my life I met several young new Christians, one of whom I had known years before in high school. (I later married him.) They were warm, real people, and they became my friends. Soon I began to hear what they were saying about God. Then they told me something I had never known, but longed for. They told me how to find Him. It wouldn't be by working harder, or accumulating "things," or through any efforts of my own. But I *would* find Him through a Person. Someone who would understand my need, meet my need, and feed my hungry spirit.

My friends urged me to give my life to Jesus Christ and let Him fill the empty places. So I did. It was simple, quiet, and very, very real. I said yes to Jesus and the God I had believed to be real, but far away, came into my life.

And what a difference He made and continues to make for me. And it all began with being made humble enough to *know* my need.

In Touch with Your Need

Until we do reach out to God, our sense of need can make us very uncomfortable. In fact, we may try to hide it or camouflage it by acting self-sufficient, even proud and arrogant. It's a strange thing about pride—often it's a cover-up for a low opinion of self.

I have a friend of long-standing, a lovely person who, when she was younger, had such a bad self-image that she almost called it quits. She was so desperately in need of inner security and peace that she was almost totally unable to give to others, even to her husband and children. Margot covered up her inner need so cleverly and with such a layer of bravado that none of us realized how empty she felt inside. In fact, she rather intimidated people, which kept her from the very relationships she longed for.

One day Margot felt a mysterious stirring within her, perhaps an answer to the prayers of her family and friends who had patiently hung in there with her. Quietly, persistently, the Holy Spirit pushed against her resistance until it cracked. Slowly, over many months, Margot gingerly reached out for help. She began coming to church, and later entered into counseling with my husband. When Louie realized how deep and long-standing her feelings of unworthiness were, he persuaded her to see a sensitive Christian psychiatrist. After more than a year, with Louie and the doctor working with her, Margot came in touch with her real need, and God was able to bring about a healing in her life. It was a miracle that culminated in a most simple way.

Margot was driving home from the psychiatrist's office one day after a session that had been a breakthrough. The Holy Spirit had convinced Margot of her need—and more— He had convinced her it was OK to be needy. Indeed, it was healthy and good. As she drove through the park she felt warmed by that light. Suddenly, she found herself saying, "Margot, you're a precious person. You're special. God loves you!"

Over and over again she said those words, until she began to cry. Finally, unable to see the road through her tears, she pulled over, stopped the car, and sat basking in God's love. Later, as Margot started the car to drive home, she did something very significant and symbolic. She reached down and fastened her seat belt. In that one simple act she was saying, "God cares, so I care...at last!"

Margot began a new life, in touch with her need for God—walking humbly with Him and able to "humbly accept the Word" planted in her. As a result, she is able now to give to her family and to others enormously! Two years ago, we experienced a heartwarming postscript to this story. On a trip west, Louie and I visited a church where we met person after person who told us how much they had been helped by a gifted, caring psychologist on the church staff . . . a woman with deep sensitivity to their problems. And yes, to our *great* joy, we discovered that person was Margot. (O God, You are *so* good!)

Humble Living

> Everyone should be quick to listen, slow to speak and slow to become angry, for man's anger does not bring about the righteous life that God desires. Therefore, get rid of all moral filth and the evil that is so prevalent, and humbly accept the Word planted in you, which can save you (James 1:19-21).

Humility is not incidental to being a good listener. And if you're a good listener, you're going to be "slow to speak"—for there's no way you can speak and listen at the same time. Neither will you be allowed to indulge in the common practice of *looking* like you are politely listening when you are really thinking about what you want to say next. Humility enables a person to be genuinely interested in other people and to *want* to hear what they say.

My friend, Becky Pippert, says that she and her husband, Wes, first met over the phone. Wes adds, "It was love at first sound." Another friend is fond of saying her husband fell in love with her "big ears," for it began the night she said, "Tell me about *you.*" Listening is a practical expression of God's love in and through our lives. When we listen to others, we demonstrate a humble quality which is part of "the righteous life that God desires."

Humility listens and is able to learn from all kinds of people. It understands and has many friends because it makes time and space in its life for others. Humility has a grateful heart and opens the way to God and happiness. On the other hand, pride stands back, fists clenched, and says, "I can do it myself."

Pride is a very subtle thing—the socially accepted sin of our day. We do tend, even as Christians, to make light of it as though it were one of the lesser evils. But Solomon, in his list of things God hates, says pride comes first:

These six things doth the Lord hate; yea, seven are an abomination unto Him: a proud look, a lying tongue, and hands that shed innocent blood, a heart that deviseth wicked imaginations, feet that be swift in running to mischief, a false witness that speaketh lies, and he that soweth discord among brethren (Prov. 6:16-19, KJV).

How does pride manifest itself in our lives? Pride makes us live very narrow lives, for it must have all the answers and get its own way. It talks too much, and *is not* a good listener. It has trouble getting along with people because it wants too much and offers too little. And most seriously, pride makes the mistake of thinking it can get along without God and takes to itself the credit that really belongs to Him.

Humility is exactly the opposite. The humble person knows he needs God's help, and he is open and eager to receive it. He humbly accepts the Word which has been planted within him. But he not only *hears* God's Word, he also receives it and acts upon it. That kind of response to God requires humble submission.

With hands outstretched and hearts open, we need to allow God's Word to sit in judgment over us. We do not have the pious and prideful privilege of choosing what part of the Word of God fits comfortably into our lives. In humility, we acknowledge that we need *all* of it. This kind of openness to God's Word and work keeps us healthily in touch with our own need, and helps us resist the lie that whispers we have none.

Steps to Humility

When people are humble, their attitudes, actions, and reactions are permeated with that special quality. They don't talk about being humble; it is simply part of them and—shadow-like—goes with them wherever they go. I think James had this view of humility, for he does not deal with humility neatly in one passage. Rather, he intertwines it with other themes as though humility were the natural companion of Christian deeds. He writes:

> Who is wise and understanding among you? Let him show it by his good life, by deeds done in the *humility* that comes from wisdom. Submit yourselves, then, to God. Resist the devil, and he will flee from you. Come near to God and He will come near to you. Wash your hands, you sinners, and purify your heart, you double-minded. *Humble* yourselves before the Lord, and He will lift you up (James 3:13; 4:7-8, 10).

Always practical and down to earth, James gives us his "how-to" section on becoming humble. In his commentary for laymen, *From Trials to Triumphs,* Derek Prime says, "There is undoubted significance in the order of the instructions given in James 4:7-9; it is important therefore that the order should be observed, and the relationship of one instruction to the other noted." Let's look at the steps to humility found in this passage.

1. *Submit yourselves, then, to God* (v. 7). Submission means letting go, telling God where we know we have done wrong, and letting Him show us areas of sin we might not have been aware of at all.

Submission and surrender are related. I cannot use the term *surrender* without thinking of our friend Kent, who is a plumber. For years of his younger life, Kent was addicted to drugs. His muddled mind led him into a life of anger, violence, and bizarre activities. That was where he lived, and his situation appeared hopeless. One day, desperate for a "fix," he sent "friends" out with his last dollars to get the drug he craved—but they never returned. Out of drugs, out of money, and out of friends, Kent hit bottom. At that moment he knew it was the end for him—*or* the beginning. From somewhere deep inside, he cried out to God for help. And God answered his call.

Still a young man, and now a member of Narcotics-Anonymous, Kent leans daily on the Lord for his strength. And the sign on the back of his pickup truck says it all: *I didn't quit! I surrendered!*

2. *Resist the devil, and he will flee from you* (v. 7). Perhaps the fact that "resist the devil" comes immediately after submission means the devil is going to be after those who are serious in their surrender to the Lord. I know it is true in my own life. Many times new Christians have told me this was true for them as well.

There was a period of time when Kent, our plumber-friend, spent every day at our house working on a project for us. Again and again in the early morning Louie and I would go to the kitchen to find him sitting at the table, his head bent over his Bible, reading and praying. He was doing what he called his "daily maintenance." "I can't make it without it," he said.

Clearly, Kent was "resisting the devil." I wish more of us had the feeling of complete dependence on God that we saw in him. The last day Kent worked for us, as he said good-bye and was about to leave the house, he took a tiny piece of paper he had folded in his wallet and handed it to me. It read: *Keep ever in mind the admission you made on the day of your profession in A.A. Namely that you are powerless and that it was only with your willingness to turn your life and will into My keeping that relief came to you.* (Kent is also a member of Alcoholics Anonymous. He wisely says, "I'll take all the support I can get.") This kind of awareness keeps Kent humble as he engages in an ongoing "resistance movement." Fortunately, he knows that Christ, to whom he has turned over his life, is "greater than the one who is in the world" (1 John 4:4).

3. *Come near to God* (v. 8). Coming near to God means spending time with Him, listening to Him, praying to Him, living the life of faith as we abide in Him. "Coming near" must please God, for it demonstrates our love and eagerness to be with Him. Hebrews 11:6 tells us God "rewards those who earnestly seek Him" and the reward is His nearness in return.

God's nearness is certain to bring a sense of humility to our lives as we become aware of the beauty of His pres-

138 § *Living True*

ence. Some of us may feel rather smug from time to time when we measure our lives alongside someone who is on the losing side of a struggle. But when we draw near to God and we see ourselves in relation to Him, *that* is something else. Humility comes from seeing ourselves in comparison to Him, close up! No room now for conceit! God keeps our egos slim, yet healthy!

4. *Wash your hands, you sinners, and purify your hearts, you double-minded* (4:8). Derek Prime says, "Our hands represent our actions. Whatever we do we tend to employ our hands." Our wrong actions must be repented of and cleansed. We have submitted, resisted the devil, and drawn near to God; now we must turn about and walk a new direction, which is what repentance means. Again, we turn to Soren Kierkegaard's words, "To be pure in heart is to *will one thing*." No more double-mindedness, but pure hearts that "will one thing"—to live God's way.

5. *Humble yourselves before the Lord, and He will lift you up* (4:10). Here James echoes a familiar biblical theme "Whoever exalts himself will be humbled, and whoever humbles himself will be exalted" (Matt. 23:12). And our Lord Jesus who spoke those words is our prime example of One who humbled Himself in the ultimate way on our behalf.

As we *begin* to understand this amazing truth, and *begin* to appropriate God's amazing grace, humility can *begin* to take root in our lives. For apart from catching at least a glimpse of the "height and depth" of Christ's love for us— and His suffering on the cross on our behalf, true humility is impossible.

Jesus said, "Blessed are the poor in spirit" (Matt. 5:3). How true—for that is where real life begins. But we are to "walk humbly with God" through *all* our days, not just as we begin the journey (Micah 6:8). And so we must learn to live with the dynamic tension of our poverty and God's resources, our weakness and His strength. We learn to trust Him, and not ourselves. And that very trusting keeps us aware of our need and makes our hearts tender and humble.

In one of the hymns I love most, Isaac Watts captures well what I am trying to say:

> When I survey the wondrous cross,
> On which the Prince of glory died,
> My richest gain I count but loss,
> And pour contempt on all my pride.

Our Father,
Teach us that to be humble, we do not have to deny our gifts or have a low opinion of ourselves—but simply be in touch with our deep and basic inner need for You. As we learn to live with this awareness, help us walk humbly with You, dear Lord, and with our brothers and sisters in life. Amen.

Is any one of you in trouble? He should pray. Is anyone happy? Let him sing songs of praise. Is any one of you sick? He should call the elders of the church to pray over him and anoint him with oil in the name of the Lord. And the prayer offered in faith will make the sick person well; the Lord will raise him up. If he has sinned, he will be forgiven. Therefore confess your sins to each other and pray for each other so that you may be healed. The prayer of a righteous man is powerful and effective.

Elijah was a man just like us. He prayed earnestly that it would not rain, and it did not rain on the land for three and a half years. Again he prayed, and the heavens gave rain, and the earth produced its crops.

My brothers and sisters, if one of you should wander from the truth and someone should bring [you] back, remember this: Whoever turns a sinner from the error of his way will save him from death and cover a multitude of sins.

TWELVE

CHURCH ALIVE: PRAYING, PRAISING, ANOINTING, AND REACHING OUT

One of my friends who is a new believer says, "Now that I'm a Christian, everyone is telling me I will be different— but how?" Her point is well taken. In some subliminal way all of us who profess Christ know that as individuals, and as a Christian body we *are* to be different. Yet, often we are simply pale replicas of those who make no claim at all to follow Christ. I can almost hear James bellowing his disapproval: "Brothers and sisters, this ought not to be so!"

In what ways, specifically, should our behavior set us apart? How are we recognized in the world as God's peculiar people? The answer is in God's Word. The Scriptures make it clear and unequivocal: we are to be people who trust Christ and not ourselves, and we are to live daily in the aura of His love and grace. The Bible also leaves no doubt we are to live with others in our heart, treating brothers and sisters in the way we ourselves would like to be treated. We are to be agents of justice in the world. As disciples of Christ we are to walk the second mile with people and go beyond justice, to freely offering "justice— surpassing grace." These are broad biblical basics of our faith. But as we take a closer look, we see that the New Testament particularly is bursting with the specifics I am looking for as well. There we find great sections that deal with characteristics, attitudes, and actions that when lived out in our lives, will make us very different indeed.

This closing paragraph in the Book of James is just such a passage. In these brief verses James admonishes his readers, then and now, to a quality of life in Christ that is deep and rich. James speaks to the individual believer—the "anys"— but always "among" others in the body of Christ. I have come to think of this as the "any—among" passage because it tells us how to function in a vital, alive church.

> Is any one among you suffering?... Is any cheer-
> ful?... Is any among you sick?... If any one among
> you wanders from the truth... (5:13-14, 19, RSV).

And so his message is not only personal, but for the church as well. And his teaching as to what we should do and be is very specific.

A Natural Response

> Is anyone among you suffering? Let him pray (5:13,
> RSV).

Many times I have heard Christians derided or put down because they do *just* that. They go to God when they are hurting or in trouble. And, of course, if that is the only time we pray, we deserve the chiding. But if we are sincere in our walk with God and then come into a time of suffering, prayer should be our natural response. This is the way God means for us to live; for He has told us that we have immediate access into His presence where "we may receive mercy and find grace to help us in our time of need" (Heb. 4:16).

I still feel very tender as I think back to the night a few years ago when my need was great and I asked for God's strength to be made perfect in my weakness. Louie and I had gone to bed rather early when, at about 2 A.M., we were awakened from a deep sleep by the ringing of the telephone. I reached the phone before Louie. It was a long-distance call from my stepfather in California. His voice was full of anguish. "Oh, dear God! Cokie, my Stella's gone— your mother just died."

Mother gone? She couldn't be! I had talked to her the day before. She wasn't feeling well, was having tests. But dead? *No,* God! No!

"Heart attack," he said.

I felt a cold mass in my chest and began to tremble. "Jim, just hold on. I'll get the first flight I can."

I was aware of his awful need and I wanted so to comfort him, but my own pain was overwhelming me. So I did the only thing I could do, the only thing that was natural and right at that moment. I fell to my knees in prayer beside our bed. Waves of sorrow washed over me as I thought of my mother, the woman who had been both mother and father to me as I grew up. The one who had so committed herself to me that, though we were poor, I had always felt secure in her love and safe in the simple home she had worked so hard to maintain.

She had been such a pal, so much fun. And my heart broke as I thought of our earthly relationship ending so abruptly, as if in the middle of a sentence. I ached to hold her hand in mine as we had always done when we were together. Everything in me cried out, "God, *help*—I can't make it unless You do!" I didn't know what to ask Him for; I could only reach out in weakness for His strength.

As I knelt there praying I was aware of a change—slowly, gently—coming over me. I felt like a warm blanket of love was being wrapped around my shivering body. The pain was still there, but I knew I would make it—and I would have strength to share with others.

As I flew to California the much needed tears began to flow, and the prayers continued. I was astonished that so much pain and peace could co-exist. God's powerful presence was with me in the days that followed as I went about taking care of the tasks of death which in their very doing were a blessing. I was qualitatively stronger than my usual self, and I knew it was God's work. Leaning on Him every moment, continuing in prayer, asking and receiving, I found "help in my time of need." The Holy Spirit did not make me *feel* less, but enabled me to handle more. I don't know what I would have done if I hadn't had prayer as a living and powerful resource in my life.

Prayer and Praise

> The prayer of a righteous man is powerful and effective. Elijah was a man just like us. He prayed earnestly that it would not rain, and it did not rain on the land for three and a half years. Again he prayed, and the heavens gave rain, and the earth produced its crops (5:16-18).

Here James lays down some ground rules for effectual prayer when he says the prayers of a righteous person are "powerful." And before we think that cuts us out, because we know we're not all that righteous, let's remember that a "righteous person" is one who is in a right relationship with God, by faith. But if James has taught us anything, it is that faith is seen in how we live—so a "righteous person" is one whose faith is demonstrated in action as well as in words.

Elijah's earnest prayers held back the rain, then called it forth. In case we think his example is not valid because he was some kind of spiritual giant, James adds that Elijah was a human being "just like us" (v. 17).

Another admonition we get from James is closely linked to prayer:

> Is anyone happy? Let him sing songs of praise (v. 13).

We are to be people and a church that sing and give praise to God! How wonderful. James calls us to be free in our expressions of joy and praise to Christ. And since "*every* good and perfect gift is from above" (1:17), who better to praise for every gift of life than God Himself?

Louie and I have a dear friend who is an infectious Christian man. You just can't be with John long without catching his joy. One day a few springs ago we were driving with him down Massachusetts Avenue. The street was lined with blossoming trees and splashes of new green everywhere. We were all "oohing and aahing" about the outrageous beauty of our city when John, who was getting more and more carried away by the moment, rolled down the window on his side of the car. Reaching one arm and his head out the window, he shook a fist at the sky and shouted, "Oh, God, You're such a show-off!"

We all laughed and joined him in his spontaneous, genuine song of praise. It is good for us to be with our friend John . . . he frees us to express the praise we feel to God. At another time and in another place, Albert Schweitzer spoke to the need for praise and warmth in our lives when he said, "There is so much coldness in our world because we are afraid to be as cordial as we really are."

My mother-in-law is another person whose life seems to be almost a living psalm. Expressions of gratitude flow so naturally from her lips, whether for some delicate, intoxicating scent, a beautiful sunset, or the tiny yet thoughtful deed of some stranger on the street. She has taught me so much about the joy and health of a sincere, natural expression of gratitude. In fact, the older I get the more liberated I feel to praise God in a variety of ways as she does, to give expression to the joy He has put in my heart . . . to "go for it" in the Lord!

James validates the rightness of this freedom in the Spirit when he says, "Is anyone happy? Let him sing songs of praise" (v. 13).

Prayer and Healing

> Is any one of you sick? He should call the elders of the church to pray over him and anoint him with oil in the name of the Lord. And the prayer offered in faith will make the sick person well; the Lord will raise him up (5:14-15).

Louie and I and our four young children were living in Bel Air, California where he had been called to begin a new church. Very late one evening just as we were about to hop into bed, the phone rang. It was David, one of our new members, a convert whose Jewish background added a richness and diversity to our little growing flock. David had not been a religious Jew, so the study of the Scriptures was a totally new experience for him; his excitement over the treasures he found there was a challenge to all of us. His fresh response to biblical truths helped us see things in a new light. And so it was on this occasion.

"Louie, I'm in bed sick."

"Sorry to hear that, Dave."

"Yeah, well, I've been reading my Bible, and here in James chapter 5 it says if I'm sick I'm supposed to call the elders, and you guys are supposed to anoint me with oil and pray for me to be healed."

There it was again. David's simple, childlike response was pushing us to reexamine where we were in relation to what the Bible said.

That was a long time ago and I can't honestly recapture the time frame or series of events that followed. I do know that Louie reviewed the biblical passages on healing and found that during His earthly ministry, Jesus stopped time and time again to heal someone on the way. Our Lord never treated those occasions as interruptions, but always as a continuation of His ministry. Clearly, Jesus was concerned for the whole person, and healing was a natural response to that concern. So in obedience, and with a bit of trembling I'm sure, Louie gathered some of the elders and together they went to David's home where they anointed him with oil and prayed, and he did get well.

Since that simple beginning, ministries of healing have been part of the ordinary life of our congregations. In the church we now serve, there is a "prayer for healing" service every 4 to 6 weeks, a time of God's quiet deep work in our midst. Some among us have discovered a personal gift of faith to pray for God's healing power, but we are seeing that healing is also a ministry given to the whole church. Healing flows from the fellowship and love of those who give themselves to each other and to prayer. At the healing service, our teaching and ruling elders anoint with oil and lay hands upon the sick, whether of mind, heart, or body. And they do this in obedience, knowing it is not the oil that is the indispensable ingredient, but the principle it symbolizes—for oil in Scripture is the symbol of the Holy Spirit.

During the teaching time that is part of each service, Louie is very clear that *God* is the Healer and He heals the sick through prayer. Healing comes through physicians' hands as well; we do not see these as opposing forces to be pitted against each other, but simply the fullest use of all God has provided for our wholeness. The point is, God is in charge. He has control over every cell in our bodies and all our illnesses and psychoses are in reach of His touch, through whatever means He chooses to use.

Our part is to believe and pray—to know God *can* heal and God *does* heal—but not always. For if God allowed us "healing upon demand," we would be putting God in a straightjacket where He would not be free to do what is best for us. In the words of my father-in-law, Dr. Louis Evans, Sr., "All death would then be arrested by our intercessions. The gates of death would never open, and the gates of glory never receive those who had won their crown" (*Make Your Faith Work*, Revell). In obedience and hope, we pray for the sick to be healed; we lean into it rather than away from it. But we always keep in mind the underlying factor of God's good and sovereign will.

> And the prayer offered in faith will make the sick person well; the Lord will raise him up. If he has sinned, he will be forgiven (v. 15).

In considering this verse it is so important for us not to generalize and say that *all* sickness comes from sin. That would not be true to Scripture (as one example among many, remember Epaphroditus who for the work of Christ was sick, "nigh unto death," Phil. 2:30, KJV). It is painful enough for a person to be ill, and how much more painful when friends imply that the sickness has come because of some wrongdoing or lack of faith. We are not to set ourselves up as judges in such matters.

But having said that, we have to be willing to see the other side. Some illness *is* the result of sin. When we knowingly and *willfully* break God's commands, they end up breaking us. For instance, when we allow ourselves to hate certain people, we may find they literally give us a "pain in the neck." When we refuse to trust God with our anxieties and concerns, that frequent knot in our stomach may become an ulcer. And when we fail to work through our anger in healthy ways, we may literally make ourselves "blind with rage."

I remember when I was a young mother nursing our babies I was amazed how quickly my emotional mood was transmitted through the milk I gave our children. If I was upset or in turmoil of any kind, those smart little rascals knew it and registered their complaint. There is no doubt about it! Our inner attitudes have physical manifestations. And when we become ill as a result, the sickness may disappear when the wrong attitude is healed and made right.

Look at these Old Testament gems of truth from the Book of Proverbs:

A crushed spirit dries up the bones (17:22).
An anxious heart weighs a man down (12:25).
The cheerful heart has a continual feast (15:5).
A merry heart does good like a medicine (17:22, KJV).

Prayer and Confession

Therefore, confess your sins to each other and pray for
each other so that you may be healed (v. 16).

Here, confession among brothers and sisters in Christ within the body of the church is encouraged. In place of "sin," the *King James Version* says "faults"—and there *is* a feeling today that confession should be limited to minor "faults," and certainly not include SINS. (That could be embarrassing!) But the word in the Greek is *harmartias,* which is the New Testament word for sins. Simply, clearly, James is telling us to be open with one another about our SINS.

We do this so little in the church today, and perhaps that is one way we limit the power of God to work in our lives as deeply as He wants and as much as we need Him to. Not that I am recommending large-scale public confession—that can get unhealthy *real* fast. But I do think confessing to the person or group affected, and to a group of trusted covenant brothers and sisters who will listen, pray, and keep us accountable in the future, is both helpful and right.

Psychologist O.H. Mowrer sees early Christianity as a small group movement where Christians made things right with God and with one another within their congregations. This practice was so powerfully redemptive and healing that Mowrer credits it with the amazing spread of the faith in those embryonic years. I think he has a good point. Confession releases power—and God's power is what we need in our churches today. Confession is painful, humbling, and difficult, so it can become a practical deterrent to sin in the future, as well as a dynamic that unites us in the present. In *Life Together,* Dietrich Bonhoeffer wrote:

> In confession, the breakthrough to community takes place. [Sin] withdraws [us] from the community . . . sin wants to remain unknown. It shuns the light. In the darkness of the unexpressed it poisons . . . in confession the light of the Gospel breaks into the darkness and seclusion of the heart . . . it is a hard struggle until sin is openly admitted. But God breaks gates of brass and bars of iron.

James admonishes us to give ourselves to confession and prayer, a powerful duo and then follows with the beautiful words: "that you may be healed" (v. 16). I've seen it happen, have had it happen, where the unburdening of a troubled spirit, and assurance of sins forgiven has brought a great cleansing and healing in my life and in the lives of those I love.

One situation I remember particularly well happened some years ago. I had harbored a bitter feeling in my heart toward a woman who had said some things that had been very painful to me. Instead of going to her and talking about it as I should have done (and would do today), I nursed my hurts, and hugged the grudge I felt against her. In my silence, the whole thing grew out of proportion in my mind and I remember waking often at night, and walking through days in what the poet E.E. Cummings calls an "undead" state. I felt drained and tired during that period of my life. Bonhoeffer's words, "The darkness of the unexpressed poisons the whole being of a person," were true for me.

Finally, I confessed my ugly feelings and touchiness to God. I asked His forgiveness and healing and expected everything to be OK. But the confession was not complete. In words I could understand, if not hear, God let me know I had to confess to the woman against whom I had sinned. I remember thinking (arguing?): *But God, she started it. She should confess to me!* I knew He wouldn't let me get away with that, for I was responsible for *my* feelings, *my* sin, not hers.

I prayed for courage, and with my heart pounding, made my way to her home and broke the silence between us. It was a struggle, but the cleansing and lifting of the burden was worth every painful moment.

I cannot say we became "bosom buddies" immediately, or ever. But we were reconciled in love, cleansed, and forgiven—and the joy and lightness of heart I felt as a result of confessing to her was profound. And it was accompanied by a kind of healing; I rested more peacefully at night, and lived more "in touch" by day. That confession, therefore, was amazingly practical for me. It was the act of spelling out my sin so that God could deal with it—and confessing to the person involved in it with me.

When we confess, we do more than admit our faults; we drop our defenses and come to grips with our inner selves. We stop blaming life, other people, parents, friends, or even God. In confession we take the blame ourselves.

Some people think they can leave sin alone, ignore it and

maybe it will go away. But neglect only makes it worse, for sin cries out for attention. Other people shy away from confession, thinking it is a preoccupation with sin. But that is a misunderstanding. Confession is God's way for us to get *rid* of sin, not dwell on it. I am an eager housecleaner, not because I take a morbid delight in dirt, but because I *like* a clean house.

And what if we refuse to confess our sins—what then? When we do not live a loving, confessing, forgiving style of life in the body of Christ, strange things begin to happen. Unconfessed sin and guilt can make us hard on ourselves and others. We develop an appetite for failure, become accident prone, lock ourselves into miserable human relationships. We punish ourselves in some way, for we are very resourceful. A woman repeatedly hospitalized with various ailments claims, "My body has been drained by inner conflicts of all power to resist disease." It is true. When we allow unconfessed sin and guilt to accumulate in our lives, it is impossible to enjoy health ourselves or impart it to others. In this light James' words, "Confess your sins to each other and pray for each other so that you may be healed," become very practical indeed!

Prayer and Restoration
Now James writes his final words of admonition to his scattered family in Christ.

> My brothers and sisters, if one of you should wander from the truth and someone should bring him back, remember this: Whoever turns a sinner away from his error will save him from death and cover many sins (vv. 19-20).

James has been talking about a quality of life for individual Christians, and for the church. He has called us to prayer, to praise, to confession, to wholeness and health. Now he ends his message almost abruptly as he focuses in on the spiritual relationship of every person with God. In his typical no-nonsense way, James emphasizes this relationship as the *ultimate* reason for our being. While all the other points are important, I think James is telling us they are lesser goals.

Our *ultimate* purpose is to
  know
   love
    serve and
     honor
      Jesus Christ.

The other factors are *part* of our life and journey in Christ, but *He* is our journey's end. The fact that James closes his message with this truth is significant. Credible, practical Christian living cannot be separated from a genuine concern for the spiritual welfare of our sisters and brothers in life. This is the *bottom* line.

But this passage is not without its problems. Verse 20 has been taken by some to mean that the one who reaches out and rescues someone for Christ will, by doing that, cover their *own* sins. But there is no way we can *earn* forgiveness of our own sins, *ever*! That is God's work.

Writing on this passage, Dr. Frank Gaebelein said:

There is only one covering for sins, and that is the atoning blood of the Lord Jesus Christ. Actually, James is saying that the believer who leads even one sinner to Christ is being used to cover the multitudinous sins of the one who has been converted. The emphasis is a completely unselfish one, beautifully characteristic of the apostle of applied Christianity, whose letter so uniquely reflects the mind of the Lord Jesus.

But this is not to say the one who reaches out does not receive a great blessing. William Barclay notes, "The highest honor God can give is bestowed upon him who leads another to God; for the one who does that does nothing less than share in the work of Jesus Christ."

And in a sense, as we reach out to others we *are* saved—from lack of concern, lovelessness, and the temptation to be silent about the riches we have in Christ. But in the ultimate sense, we are not saved by *anything* we do. We can only respond to what God has done for us which we could *never* do for ourselves.

Once that truth is settled we can go on to these verses that deal with our ministry to one another when we stray from the truth. The verb *err* which James uses means "to wander"; it is sometimes used of a ship that is driven from its course or slipping away from its mooring. It suggests a gradual, quiet, and almost imperceptible drifting away from the will of God, what some call backsliding.

A few years ago Louie and I were meeting with a group of covenant brothers and sisters, all of whom we deeply love and trust. As we were sharing—"logging-in" we call it—it became clear that many of us had been slowly, "almost imperceptibly" moving away from the truth. Not that we had left the Lord in any overt way, or had been "caught in a sin" (Gal. 6:1), but as we confronted one another, and confessed to one another, it became clear that almost to a person we had been slowly "drifting" from the first love of our lives. All of us were involved in some Christian, church, or para-church vocations and it was our "busyness," our "work for the Lord," all the "good things" we were doing *for* Him that had become our excuse for neglecting our primary relationship *with* Him. And it had happened so subtly, just like a boat slowly, silently drifting away from its mooring.

That evening turned out to be a powerful night as we prayed for each other and called one another back from the "error of our ways" (the barrenness of our too busy lives), to "the truth" of life in Christ as revealed in the Scriptures. "Thy Word is truth" (John 17:17, KJV); God means for us to live by that truth, to "pay close attention to what we have heard, lest we drift away from it" (Heb. 2:1, RSV). I will always be grateful to those friends who trusted the group enough that night to be vulnerable in exposing the "error of their ways" and caring enough to challenge the rest of us to do the same. The honesty and love among us enabled

154 § *Living True*

healing and recommitment to flow.

"Speaking the truth in love" (Eph. 4:15) is one of the ways we reach out to one another when we are erring. That same love not only helps a sister or brother get honest about what is wrong in their lives, but it is there afterward to flood into that person's life with forgiveness and support.

Another way we can work to rescue the "drifter" among us is through prayer. James does not mention prayer in this passage, but in the preceding verses he has told us to pray for our times of trouble and illness, so it follows that he means for us to pray for our friends who have wandered from God. And our prayers will make a difference! James implies it, and Scripture confirms it again and again! Not only does prayer influence *our* hearts as we pray, but there is an effect on the person for whom we pray as well. Not that we can ever *push* a friend back to God, nor should we try. But our loving prayers can do much to make the way ready for the right response; prayer's lifting power can draw a person into the aura of awareness where they can experience God's love and grace for themselves. I cannot tell you just how it happens, but having experienced it many times I can affirm that the "divine propulsion" of prayer *really* works!

While it is clear that James is speaking to believers in verse 19 ("If *one of you* should wander from the truth"), I don't feel we are doing an injustice to his teaching if we apply this verse to unbelievers as well. If *we* need to reach out to one another when one of us drifts away from God and His ways, how important it is to also reach out to those who have never known His love in the first place. In fact, from God's perspective I wonder if that isn't the most important reaching out He has for us to do?

As humans we get so caught up in physical death, the leave-taking that occurs when a person's soul is separated from their body. And it's so natural, so human, to hurt when we are separated physically from ones we love. God understands and *cares* about our pain, and He ministers to us powerfully in our times of mourning. Yet, God does not seem to be enormously concerned about that physical death. The death He seems *most* concerned about is the spiritual death that takes place when a person's soul is separated from Him because of sin. I tend to forget how gravely God considers this and confess to Him, and to you, that I am not as eagerly involved in reaching out to those who do not know Him as I feel He would have me be.

Even now I think of a friend who, by her own admission, is not a believer. We share mutual concerns in our city, and enjoy working and spending time together. She is one of those good persons who *seems* to get along without religion; she is dear and loving. But there is a sadness about her—and I know why. Yet I have not reached out to her for Christ.

Oh, she knows I am a Christian and she teases me about being her "out to save the world" friend. But I have never picked up on it and told her *who* it is who makes me care about the world in the first place. More specifically, I have never asked her if she would like to know Him too.

But I believe our relationship has paved the way, and now I must go beyond our human friendship. I want to "live true" by reaching out to her in the ultimate sense. I am eager to share the unconditional love of Jesus Christ with her, and offer her the opportunity to choose Him for herself.

Yes, this study of James has touched my life in many ways. I knew it would. James' closing passage has convinced me in a fresh way that when we touch a soul for Christ, we touch eternity. And his final words, "If one of you should wander from the truth and someone should bring him back," has stirred a deep longing in my heart. *Lord, let me be that "someone" for some others, I pray.*

James, the apostle of applied Christianity, brings us to his bottom line—the relationship between God and His people. And in his ever practical way, James, the brother of our Lord, urges us to live our faith by reaching out to others in

Christ's name.

> What regret would then be mine,
> When I meet my Lord Divine,
> If I've wasted all the talents He did lend.
> If no soul to me can say,
> "I am glad you passed my way,
> For it was you who told me of the sinner's Friend"
> (*Make Your Faith Work,* pp. 58-59).